Labour and the Politics of Disloyalty in Belfast, 1921–39

Christopher J. V. Loughlin

Labour and the Politics of Disloyalty in Belfast, 1921–39

The Moral Economy of Loyalty

Christopher J. V. Loughlin
Belfast, UK

ISBN 978-3-319-71080-8   ISBN 978-3-319-71081-5   (eBook)
https://doi.org/10.1007/978-3-319-71081-5

Library of Congress Control Number: 2017964190

This Palgrave Macmillan imprint is published by Springer Nature
The registered company is Springer International Publishing AG
The registered company address is: Gewerbestrasse 11, 6330 Cham, Switzerland

For the Working Class.

PREFACE

The 1960s and 1970s witnessed a plethora of Marxisant studies of Northern Ireland and the so-called 'unfinished' Irish Revolution. Ireland, like much of the Western world, was affected by the radical 1960s. However, the neo-liberal counter-revolutions, starting in the mid-1970s, saw the ebbing of this radical wave. It is only now, in 2018, that we are beginning to see the emergence of new, radical, critical studies of Irish society and politics: the Irish New Wave. The present study, *Labour and the Politics of Disloyalty in Belfast, 1921–39: The Moral Economy of Loyalty*, picks up the threads left by previous Marxisant studies about the north of Ireland. However, the methodology pioneered in this study owes an important debt to the work of E. P. Thompson, Ellen Meiksins Wood, Robert Brenner and the school of 'Political Marxism'.

Labour and the Politics of Disloyalty is a 'history from below' of the labour movement in the city of Belfast in the aftermath of the partition of Ireland. It is a social history of the politics of Belfast labour and applies methodology from history, sociology and political science. The book questions previous analysis, which has asserted the centrality of religion and sectarian conflict in the establishment of Northern Ireland. *Labour and the Politics of Disloyalty* suggests that political division and violence were key to the foundation and maintenance of the democratic *ancien régime* in Northern Ireland. The study interrogates the academic consensus that politics 'ossified' in the province during the inter-war period and moves past the 'populist' and 'anti-populist' designation utilised by Paul Bew, Peter Gibbon and Henry Patterson. It utilises a broad, 'social' approach to analyse the politics of Belfast labour. The book is complementary to recent work on Irish labour, including literary and socio-economic history published by Seán Byers, David Convery, Bryce Evans, Adrian Grant, Peter Leary, Emmet O'Connor and Michael Pierse. It is similarly complementary to the new wave of gender and women's history which developed in Ireland from the 1970s. Outstanding scholars in this area include Marie Coleman, Virginia Crossman, Elaine Farrell, J. G. V. McGaughey, Diane Urquhart and Olwen Purdue.

Labour and the Politics of Disloyalty is a theoretically engaged work which places the labour movement within historiographical debate on the Irish Revolution, the inter-war history of Northern Ireland and the 'failure' of class politics on the island. It is a revisionist, thematic series of case studies of the labour movement in Belfast in 1921–39, and it examines important topics such as political violence, sectarianism, class, gender and labour's relationship to the political culture established in Northern Ireland. The book concludes that the Belfast labour movement balanced precariously within a binary, 'zero sum', politics, or, as the book describes it, 'the moral economy of loyalty'. This 'moral economy of loyalty' was the means by which the Ulster Unionist Party (UUP) of Northern Ireland discriminated against all those considered 'disloyal'.

Labour, in the city of Belfast, was excluded from the loyal political culture constructed in the region by the UUP governance of Northern Ireland. The labour movement as a whole was—alongside Catholics, republicans and nationalists—considered 'disloyal', suspect and liable to political discrimination. Labour was unable to overturn the dominance of local politics by the UUP, but the present book demonstrates that this was in large part due to the political malpractice established by the local elite. *Labour and the Politics of Disloyalty* does not seek to speak on behalf of those who suffered at the hands of the winners of local politics. This slim study instead seeks to rescue the local labour movement from the 'enormous condescension of posterity'. The extent to which the present author has succeeded is, of course, a matter for the reader.

Belfast, UK   Christopher J. V. Loughlin

ACKNOWLEDGEMENTS

I would first like to acknowledge the support of the Loughlin family: Victor senior, Glenda, Victor junior, Grahame, Alexander and Rosemary. This book could not have been written without the help of the entire family. I also wish to thank and acknowledge friends, comrades and the wider left. There is an Irish New Wave developing today and it is a product of the sacrifice and importance of those comrades and friends.

I also wish to acknowledge an Arts and Humanities Research Council studentship (2009–12). This studentship was based at Queen's University Belfast and resulted in the PhD thesis on which this book is based, 'The Political Culture of the Belfast Labour Movement, 1924–39'. I also wish to acknowledge and thank Professor Fearghal McGarry and Professor Graham Walker. Professor McGarry, in particular, pushed and developed the work presented in this book. The library staff at the McClay Library, Queen's University Belfast, have also been of great help and assistance. Particular thanks must be given to the professional help and assistance of Andrew, Constance, Diarmuid, Eoin and Victoria.

I would like to acknowledge permission to reproduce the article, 'The Moral Economy of Loyalty: Labour, Law, and the State in Northern Ireland, 1921–1939' by Christopher John Victor Loughlin. This article originally appeared in *Labour History Review*, lxxxii, issue 1, pp. 1–22. The copyright for this article is owned by the present author and Liverpool University Press. I wish to acknowledge their permission to reproduce this article as chapter four of the present book. This article is reproduced with permission of the licensor through PLSclear.

I would also like to acknowledge permission to quote from material which is housed at the Public Record Office of Northern Ireland (PRONI). I also acknowledge permission from the Ulster Unionist Council (UUC) and PRONI to quote from the Ulster Unionist Labour Association minutes contained in the UUC papers at PRONI, D/1327/11/4/1. I further acknowledge permission from PRONI to quote from the records of Sam Napier, D/3702/B/4A-4G. I also wish to acknowledge permission to quote from the minute book of the Central Women's Section of the Northern Ireland Labour Party housed at PRONI, D/3311/1/1. I further wish to acknowledge permission to quote from the Harry Midgley papers at PRONI, D/4089/4/1/36. Last, I wish to acknowledge permission to quote from a series of Ministry of Home Affairs (HA) (Northern Ireland) files held at PRONI. Those HA files, for which permission was granted to quote from by PRONI, are HA/32/1/546, HA/32/8/276, HA/32/1/550, HA/32/1/551, HA/32/1/553, HA/32/1/619, HA/32/1/554, HA/5/1301, HA/32/1/490, HA/32/1/516, HA/32/1/598 and HA/32/1/562.

Finally, I would like to acknowledge permission to quote from the Communist Party of Ireland papers, courtesy of Dublin City Library & Archive. This relates to file, box 4/016.

CONTENTS

ABBREVIATIONS

AEU	Amalgamated Engineering Union
ASW	Amalgamated Society of Woodworkers
ATGWU	Amalgamated Transport & General Workers' Union
CAIN	Conflict Archive on the Internet
GAA	Gaelic Athletic Association
ICWPA	International Class War Prisoners Aid
ILP	Independent Labour Party
INTO	Irish National Teachers' Organisation
IPP	Irish Parliamentary Party
IRA	Irish Republican Army
ITGWU	Irish Transport and General Workers' Union
ITUC	Irish Trades' Union Congress
ITUC & LP	Irish Trades' Union Congress & Labour Party
IUWM	Irish Unemployed Workers' Movement
IWWU	Irish Women Workers' Union
NCCL	National Council of Civil Liberties
NCLC	National Council of Labour Colleges
NICRA	Northern Ireland Civil rights Association
NILP	Northern Ireland Labour Party
NISP	Northern Ireland Socialist Party
NUR	National Union of Railwaymen
PRONI	Public Records Office of Northern Ireland
PUP	Progressive Unionist Party
RUC	Royal Ulster Constabulary
STV	Single Transferable Vote
TOSI	Textile Operatives' Society of Ireland
UPL	Ulster Protestant League

USSR	Union of Soviet Socialist Republics
UTU	Ulster Teachers' Union
UULA	Ulster Unionist Labour Association
UUP	Ulster Unionist Party
UVF	Ulster Volunteer Force
UWTU	Ulster Workers' Trade Union
UWUC	Ulster Women's Unionist Council
WEA	Workers' Education Association
WTUL	Women's Trade Union League

LIST OF FIGURES

LIST OF TABLES

Labour and the Politics of Disloyalty in Belfast, 1921–39: The Moral Economy of Loyalty

Abstract This chapter sets the stage for the thematic case study approach of *Labour and the Politics of Disloyalty in Belfast, 1921–39*. It assesses the historiography on the establishment of Northern Ireland, the labour movement in the region and its relationship to the Irish revolution. It defines terms utilised in the case studies. The chapter argues that whilst communal demarcation was demonstrated in religious, ethnic and colonial terms, the principal issue in Northern Ireland was political conflict and violence; this resulted in the establishment of a 'moral economy of loyalty'. Northern Ireland was a peculiar state which established a democratic *ancien régime*. Finally, it situates *The Moral Economy of Loyalty* as sympathetic to the 'social interpretation' of the Irish revolution.

Keywords Labour • Disloyalty • Belfast • Moral economy • Loyalty

The present slim volume originates from a PhD thesis, 'The Political Culture of the Belfast Labour Movement, 1924–39', funded by the Arts and Humanities Research Council and conducted at Queen's University Belfast in 2009–13. In that thesis, 'political culture' was utilised as the methodological framework to investigate the record of the inter-war Belfast labour movement. Robert Kelley, in an influential description, described the difference between politics and political culture as 'the difference between reporting the flow of play in a particular sport setting and describing the larger framework that sets up its overall nature: the rules of the game'.[1] It also involves, according to Lawrence Black, 'ordinary and elite political activity, activists and spectators'.[2] Political culture is therefore an attempt to analyse something more fundamental than politics; the concept is used to understand how the 'rules' of politics are conceptualised, measured and understood by individuals and groups. During the PhD thesis, it became clear that 'political culture' was a phrase to describe the constitution of the 'political'.[3] Finally, the present volume being the result, it became evident that previous analysis was overly harsh on the politics of labour in inter-war Belfast and the wider lack of development of class politics in Northern Ireland. But what, exactly, do we mean by 'labour'?

Andrew Finlay has argued that the Northern Ireland Labour Party (NILP) should be examined as part of the broader labour movement rather than as a purely electoral party.[4] The case studies presented below are sympathetic to Finlay's view. They attempt to examine *both* the organised political and industrial expression of the labour movement and the wider experience of working-class people. The first criterion for inclusion was evidence produced by political parties consisting of working-class people or with a specific orientation to the working class. On this basis, evidence from the NILP, the Belfast Independent Labour Party, the Northern Ireland Socialist Party and communists was examined. Furthermore, material from the Ulster Unionist Labour Association was considered because of their orientation to recruit working-class Unionists to the Ulster Unionist Party (UUP). Second, evidence from institutions and organisations which represented industrial working-class concerns was examined. For example, source material from trade unions, organisations of the unemployed and the Belfast Trades Council was examined.

---

[1] Robert Kelley quoted in R. P. Formisano, 'The Concept of Political Culture', *Journal of Interdisciplinary History*, 31 (Winter 2001), 393–426, (415).

[2] Lawrence Black, *The Political Culture of the Left in Affluent Britain, 1951–64: Old Labour, New Britain?* (Basingstoke: Palgrave Macmillan, 2003), p. 2.

[3] The case studies, which make up the rest of this book, are an attempted 'social history of the political'; it has not been possible, however, in this short work to lay out a detailed investigation of this methodology. Further research will investigate this topic. For further theoretical considerations, see C. J. V. Loughlin, 'Representing Labour: Notes Towards a Political and Cultural Economy of Irish Working-Class Experience', in *A History of Irish Working-Class Writing* ed. by Michael Pierse (Cambridge: Cambridge University Press, 2017), pp. 57–71.

[4] Andrew Finlay, *Governing Ethnic Conflict: Consociation, Identity and the Price of Peace* (Abingdon: Routledge, 2011), p. 93.

The book utilises a historical case study approach to analyse the Belfast labour movement during the inter-war period. The archival sources available, however, are limited because of the destruction caused in Belfast by the Second World War. The book has therefore relied on both public and archival sources. These sources consist primarily of newspapers, such as the *Belfast Newsletter*, *Belfast Telegraph*, *Irish News* and *Northern Whig*. Left-wing newspapers of the period—for example, *The Labour Opposition of Northern Ireland*, *The Voice of Labour* and *The Irish Democrat*—have also been used as a significant source. Newspapers tended to either glorify the role of the left or alternatively demonise it because they were produced either by the left or their opponents. Government sources from the period, especially police reports, have also been used extensively. The origins of these sources—official, private and archival—require that the historian handle the evidence with care and diligence.

This book is, however, an examination of the political literature produced by the Belfast working class. Therefore, broader cultural and literary sources were utilised at a minimum.[5] These included such important topics as the Co-operative movement in Belfast, represented primarily by the Belfast Co-operative Society Ltd. This body had a mass membership in Belfast during the period,[6] intervened in local politics,[7] and saw significant co-operation between activists who identified as Labour, Unionist and Nationalist.[8] Similarly, this book does not examine adult education represented by local branches of the Workers' Education Association (WEA)[9] and the National Council of Labour Colleges (NCLC).[10] Both of these

[5] These case studies, on the inter-war Belfast working class, should be supplemented with the consideration of Irish working-class literature in Michael Pierse, *Writing Ireland's Working Class: Dublin after O'Casey* (Basingstoke: Palgrave Macmillan, 2010); *A Cambridge History of Irish Working-Class Writing* ed. by Michael Pierse.

[6] The Belfast Co-operative Society Ltd was founded in 1889 and had 21,300 members in Belfast by 1919 and 49,526 by 1937; the records of the society can be accessed at the Public Records Office of Northern Ireland, Belfast, Northern Ireland (PRONI), Records of the Belfast Co-Operative Society Ltd, the Lisburn Co-operative Society Ltd and the Irish Co-operative Society Ltd., 1889–1983, D/3895.

[7] *Belfast Telegraph*, 14 Jan. 1927.

[8] Patrick Bolger, *The Irish Co-Operative Movement: Its History and Development* (Dublin: Institute of Public Administration, 1977), p. 141.

[9] The Belfast branch of the WEA was associated with the extra-mural department of Queen's University Belfast and its records are kept at PRONI, Papers of the Workers' Educational Association, 1907–2003, D/4465.

[10] Andrew Boyd has written an interesting account of the NCLC in Ireland; see Andrew Boyd, *Fermenting the Elements: The National Council of Labour Colleges in Ireland, 1924–64* (Belfast: Donaldson Archives, 1999).

bodies provided education to working-class adults in Belfast, though with different objectives. The WEA provided classic, liberal and non-political education, while the NCLC provided explicitly left-wing education, much like the Plebs League in Britain. At least one Socialist Sunday school existed in Belfast during the inter-war period, but again this topic was not investigated. Last, the influence of culture and literature on the Belfast labour movement was not examined. These omissions include individuals who were involved in labour activities at the time, such as John Hewitt, or who grew up in Belfast during the period, such as Sam Hanna Bell. These areas await further study and have been utilised only when they seemed particularly appropriate.[11]

The introduction below is a political narrative and discussion of the early history of the Northern Ireland state. It charts the development of the mass tradition of loyalty and the regional political culture which was formalised in the 1920s with the establishment of the state. The first section of this chapter narrates some of the historiography related to the Tory and Ulster rebellion before the First World War; some of the effects of war and revolution in Ireland; the revolutionary events in 1918–21; and the counter-revolution(s) in Ireland from 1921 to 1923. The second section of the chapter reviews the historiography related to the foundation and consolidation of the Northern Ireland state, 1921–39. It sets the historiographical and political context for the Belfast labour movement. The case studies to be presented in this book are an attempted 'social history of the political'.[12] The extent to which the author has succeeded must be left to the judgement of the reader.

1.1   SECTION I: THE FOUNDATIONS OF NORTHERN IRELAND

1.1.1   *The Mass Tradition of Loyalty*

The reckless rodomontade at Blenheim in the early summer as developed and amplified in this Ulster campaign, furnishes for the future a complete Grammar of Anarchy. The possession of a conscience and a repugnance to obey inconvenient or objectionable laws are not the monopoly of the Protestants of the northeast of Ireland. This new dogma, countersigned as

[11] See footnote 5 above.
[12] See footnote 3 above.

it now is, by all the leading men of the Tory party, will be invoked, and rightly invoked, cited, and rightly cited, called in aid, and rightly called in aid, whenever the spirit of lawlessness, fed and fostered by a sense whether of real or imaginary injustice, takes body and shape, and claims to stop the ordered machinery of a self-governing society.

H. H. Asquith, Liberal Prime Minister of the UK, 1908–15, speaking on the 5th October 1912.[13]

From 1801, Ireland was in legislative union with Great Britain. In 1886 and again in 1893, however, British politics was wracked by dispute over Home Rule for Ireland. Liberal Prime Minister Gladstone's conversion to Home Rule destroyed the bipartisan consensus of Victorian British politics on Ireland.[14] The first Home Rule bill was defeated in the Commons, whilst the second was vanquished by the House of Lords in 1893. Over the next decade, the Liberal Party was eclipsed by the Tories, a situation radically altered with the 'Liberal landslide' at the January 1906 general election. The new Liberal government proceeded to reform pensions and industrial relations. These changes were greeted hyperbolically as revolutionary by those on the right of British and Irish politics.[15]

In January 1906, the Liberal Party won the UK general election by a landslide; this was to be the high tide of Edwardian Liberal, radical, and social reform. Augustine Birrell was appointed chief secretary for Ireland in 1907 by the Liberal government, the chief secretary being the direct representative of the British government in Ireland. Birrell's tenure was, ultimately, a disaster. The British imperial state in Ireland was symbolically weakened by the separatists' Rising of Easter 1916, and the Royal Commission on the Easter Rising blamed lax liberal governance of Ireland, and Birrell in particular, as responsible for these seditious events. The Unionist W. A. Phillips, the first historian of the Irish revolution, concurred and blamed the Liberal government and Birrell for 'the incubation of revolt'.[16] However, it was the context initiated by the constitutional crisis of the 'Peoples' Budget' which made Ireland, again, a key area of dispute in British politics.

---

[13] As quoted in 'Members of the War Cabinet and Their Friends', *The Complete Grammar of Anarchy* (Dublin and London: Maunsel and Co., 1918), p. 17.

[14] Ronan Fanning, *Fatal Path: British Government and Irish Revolution, 1910–1922* (London: Faber and Faber, 2013), pp. 9–11.

[15] The extent to which the 1906 Liberal government created a welfare state is still debated.

[16] W. A. Phillips, *The Revolution in Ireland, 1906–23* (2nd ed., London and Dublin: Longmans, Green & Co., 1926), p. 45.

H. H. Asquith became prime minister in April 1908, succeeding Henry Campbell-Bannerman, who died later that month. David Lloyd George, the rising radical star of the Liberal cabinet, became the new Chancellor of the Exchequer. The House of Lords, however, rejected Lloyd George's 'People's Budget' in 1909. The budget, which was necessary to finance both social reform at home and expansion of the navy, was unwisely rejected by the Lords. In consequence, two general elections took place in 1910 and this changed the topography of British politics. The Irish Parliamentary Party (IPP) held the balance of power at Westminster and the scene was set for 'the strange death of liberal England'.[17] With the removal of the Lords' veto by the 1911 Parliament Act, it looked certain that a Liberal government, with IPP backing, would pass a Home Rule Act. It was in response to the events of 1910 and 1911 that Irish and British Unionism rebelled, unleashing what Prime Minister Asquith described as 'the complete Grammar of Anarchy'.

The 'Third Home Rule Crisis', 1911–14, shaped the contours of twentieth-century Irish and British politics: Unionism, within Ireland, was regionalised, and Ulster became the key bastion of the 'Tory rebellion'.[18] Loyalty became, at this stage, the 'invented tradition' of Ulster Unionism.[19] The Tory Party, under the leadership of Andrew Bonar Law from 1911, encouraged and co-operated in the Ulster Unionist campaign against home rule for Ireland. The Parliament Act itself may have encouraged further Tory and Unionist resistance to Home Rule; the Lords' could now merely delay legislation rather than veto it as previously. As part of this escalation, in September 1912 approximately half the adult Protestant population of Ulster signed the Solemn League and Covenant. This was, perhaps, the most successful ethnic mobilisation in history.[20] The Ulster Volunteer Force was founded in January 1913, and the machinery of an

[17] George Dangerfield, *The Strange Death of Liberal England* (original ed. 1935, New York: Capricorn Books, 1961).

[18] Chapter 2 is titled 'Tory Rebellion', George Dangerfield, *The Strange Death of Liberal England*, p. 78. Recently, Ronan Fanning, alongside many others, has claimed that Ulster Unionist resistance to Home Rule in 1911–14 was 'the Unionist revolution'. Ronan Fanning, *Fatal Path*, p. 2. The present author prefers Dangerfield's designation of a 'Tory rebellion'.

[19] *The Invention of Tradition* ed. by Eric Hobsbawm and Terence Ranger (Cambridge: Cambridge University Press, 1983).

[20] For discussion of the extent of mobilisation of Ulster's Protestant population for the Covenant, see Liam Kennedy, *Unhappy the Land: The Most Oppressed People Ever, the Irish?* (Sallins, Co. Kildare: Merrion Press, 2016), p. 131 (pp. 169–70).

Ulster Provisional Government was established, to come into operation if Home Rule became law.[21] The militarisation of Tory rebellion was matched by the formation of the Irish Volunteers and Irish Citizens' Army in November 1913; the British imperial state in Ireland now faced severe crisis.[22] This confrontation was compounded by the 'Curragh Mutiny' and successful gun-running by both Nationalists and Unionists in Ireland in the first half of 1914. Civil war in Ireland was averted only by the onset of the First World War, for Britain, on the 4th August 1914.[23] The war, or so it appeared, re-unified Ireland behind British rule.[24] The war, however, exacerbated political differences between the islands, and within just three years of the end of the First World War, the UK state was no longer a 'victor' state. By the end of 1921, the UK state was a successor regime.

1.1.2   The Birth of the Modern Irelands

The First World War, in the short term, helped to avert civil war in Ireland, but the Easter Rising and the Battle of the Somme in 1916 were interpreted as the blood sacrifice of each respective political bloc within Ireland.[25] The events of 1916 and the continued pressure of war stimulated the development of the Irish revolution. This revolution was made explicit by the replacement of the IPP as the major Irish nationalist party by Sinn Féin at the 1918 UK general election. The Sinn Féin

[21] A. T. Q. Stewart, *The Ulster Crisis* (London: Faber, 1967), p. 78; Tim Bowman, *Carson's Army: The Ulster Volunteer Force, 1910–22* (Manchester: Manchester University Press, 2007).

[22] See Niall Whelehan, 'The Irish Revolution, 1912–23', in *The Oxford Handbook of Modern Irish History* ed. by Alvin Jackson (Oxford: Oxford University Press, 2014), pp. 621–44; and Marie Coleman, *The Irish Revolution, 1917–23* (Basingstoke: Routledge, 2013).

[23] In September 1914, a Home Rule Act for Ireland was passed but suspended until the end of the war. At this stage, it was still unclear how the act would be implemented or the Ulster issue resolved.

[24] For Ireland and the First World War, see D. Fitzpatrick, 'Militarism in Ireland, 1900–22', in *A Military History of Ireland* ed. by Thomas Bartlett and Keith Jeffery (Cambridge: Cambridge University Press, 1996), pp. 379–406; Keith Jeffery, *Ireland and the Great War* (Cambridge: Cambridge University Press, 2000); *Ireland and the Great War: A War to Unite us All?* ed. by Adrian Gregory and Senia Paseta (Manchester: Manchester University Press, 2002).

[25] See J. G. V. McGaughey, *Ulster's Men: Protestant Unionist Masculinities and Militarization in the North of Ireland, 1912–1923* (Montréal: McGill-Queen's University Press, 2012). The issue of 'blood sacrifice' is still a matter of debate within Irish revolutionary studies.

MPs constituted themselves Dáil Éireann, and, in opposition to the British imperial state in Ireland, the separatist republican revolution was established in fact over the next two years.[26]

As both cause and consequence, the December 1918 general election in the UK was revolutionary. As a result of the Representation of the People Act (1918), the electorate was approximately three times larger in Ireland by comparison with the general election of December 1910. The election also demonstrated the collapse of support for the British imperial state in Ireland and the 'middle ground' of Irish politics. The newly enlarged electorate returned Sinn Féin throughout much of Ireland, but the north-east, in contrast, returned a significant number of UUP MPs. The political, violent confrontation, which had been averted pre-1914, now returned with a vengeance. The establishment of alternative structures of power in Ireland in 1919 gave political, administrative and military form to the Irish revolution. The Irish revolution's defeat of the British imperial state was sealed with the signing of the Treaty in December 1921.

However, during the chaotic post-war period, all of Europe shuddered under the impact of war, rebellion and revolution. In Britain, similarly, there were radical demands for political and social reform, whilst Ireland became gripped by rebellion, revolution and counter-revolutions. Political radicalism intersected with economics as a boom occurred in the UK as consumer demand fuelled economic expansion.[27] Belfast and the north had not participated in the anti-conscription campaign in Ireland in April 1918, but the next year, in January and February 1919, workers demanded a 44-hour week in heavy engineering. The workers of Belfast went on strike alongside 'red' Clydeside. Belfast was crippled for two weeks as services were paralysed, but by the end of February 1919, workers had returned to work with a partial victory.[28] Mayday 1919 also occasioned a

[26] The academic orthodoxy accepts the period as involving *political revolution*; however, it is arguably the extent to which *social revolution* occurred which divides analysis. The present author accepts the former and is open about the extent of the latter during the Irish revolution.

[27] Enforced saving during the war had restricted consumption; this changed decisively in 1919 and 1920.

[28] For in-depth discussions of these events, see Austen Morgan, *Labour and Partition: The Belfast Working Class, 1905–23* (London: Pluto Press, 1991); Henry Patterson, *Class Conflict and Sectarianism: The Protestant Working Class and the Belfast Labour Movement, 1868–1920* (Belfast: Blackstaff Press, 1980); Conor Kostick, *Revolution in Ireland: Popular Militancy*

march of approximately 100,000 people and a colourful display at Ormeau Park. In the January 1920 urban elections, Labour and trade union candidates won seats across the north (in Belfast, Lurgan and Lisburn, for example).[29] However, the boom and upsurge in left-wing militancy in 1918–20 were short-lived.

The changed circumstances of the post-war years, the development of a violent, militant republican campaign and the unresolved Ulster question convinced the British government of the need for a new Irish policy. The result was the Government of Ireland Act (1920), which partitioned Ireland into two separate Parliaments and administrations. This settlement remains the basis of the present border between Northern Ireland and the Republic of Ireland.[30] The Government of Ireland Act (1920) was the constitutional basis for the devolved administration of British rule through the state of Northern Ireland and this remained the case until it was repealed by the Good Friday Agreement (1998).[31] However, the southern state, which was to be set up by the Government of Ireland Act, was abortive and was superseded by the Treaty of December 1921 between the British government and representatives of Dáil Éireann. The treaty established the Irish Free State, a form of dominion rather than home rule, and following the Civil War of 1922 and 1923, the southern Irish state was consolidated.[32] The two states which emerged in Ireland, therefore, represented a messy compromise, shaped by militarism, revolution, counter-revolution and war. The newly established Northern Ireland state, for example, was shaped by the invented tradition of loyalty, Asquith's memorably described 'complete Grammar of Anarchy', and the pressure(s) of modern war and revolution(s).

1917 to 1923 (Cork: Cork University Press, 2009); A. F. Parkinson, *Belfast's Unholy War: The Troubles of the 1920s* (Dublin: Four Courts Press, 2004).

[29] Conor McCabe, 'The Irish Labour Party and the 1920 Local Elections', *Saothar*, 35 (2010), 7–20.

[30] The production of state space in Ireland is admirably documented in Paul Murray, *The Irish Boundary Commission and Its Origins, 1886–1925* (Dublin: University College Dublin Press, 2011). This should be supplemented with the recent important work on the border by Peter Leary, *Unapproved Routes: Histories of the Irish Border, 1922–1972* (Oxford: Oxford University Press, 2016).

[31] 'The Belfast Agreement: Section 2: Constitutional Issues: Annex A' <https://www.gov.uk/government/uploads/system/uploads/attachment_data/file/136652/agreement.pdf> [accessed 2 Feb. 2017].

[32] From 1937, and the adoption of a new constitution, known as Éire; Republic of Ireland Act, 1948, from 1949, officially, the Republic of Ireland.

The radicalism of the immediate post-war years was reversed in the summer of 1920 and this involved a number of counter-revolutions. Beginning in July 1920, Loyalists expelled 'disloyalists' from work and home.[33] Sir Edward Carson's speech on the 12th of July served as the pretext for this violence and conflict but was also a reaction to the escalation of the Irish Republican Army (IRA) campaign against the British authorities in southern Ireland. In retaliation for the violence in the north, the Belfast Boycott was called in the south of Ireland on 6 August 1920. Politics and economics here intersected to produce the border in Ireland. The Northern Ireland state was also therefore constituted during a period of explicit political reaction if not as the expression of such reaction itself. It combined 'old traditions', such as the history of Protestantism and loyalty in Ireland, with 'new contexts',[34] such as the border and the regionalisation of Northern Ireland as the solution to the 'Irish Question' in British politics. The Northern Ireland state which was founded in 1921 was *both ancien régime* and 'modern' product of war and revolution. But why and how was the state founded in that year?

The Northern Ireland state was established amidst the contexts of war, revolution and counter-revolutions. The Government of Ireland Act (1920) granted a devolved parliament and cabinet to Northern Ireland. Powers were devolved incrementally and in preparation for the formation of a Northern Ireland government. On Empire Day, 24 May 1921, the first Northern Ireland general election was held. The UUP emerged as the largest party, with 40 out of 52 seats in the Northern Ireland House of Commons, followed by the Nationalists (the remnants of the IPP in the north of Ireland) and Sinn Féin with six seats each. The UUP, however, never lost an election to the Northern Ireland parliament over the next 50 years and administered the state without interruption. The Government of Ireland Act (1920) granted safeguards for minorities, such as Single Transferable Vote (STV) proportional representation for local government and parliamentary elections. But the UUP government used political violence as a rationale to remove such protections and proceeded to centralise political power.[35] The political

---

[33] See Chap. 2 below.

[34] The phrases 'old traditions' and 'new contexts' can be found in E. P. Thompson, *The Making of the English Working Class* (re-issued 1980 ed., London: Penguin Classics, 2013), p. 27.

[35] STV proportional representation was used for elections to ensure the representation of minorities in both new jurisdictions in Ireland. It was replaced in Northern Ireland by 'simple

violence of the IRA, alongside Irish Nationalist and republican refusal to recognise the state, saw the UUP administration introduce draconian law and order policies, suspend local authorities and further consolidate the state. This was bolstered by the development of the Belfast Boycott, in the rest of Ireland, in response to the violence of 1920 in east Ulster. The state which thus emerged in Northern Ireland was peculiar and Janus-faced: relatively modern, industrial and commercialised yet also an *ancien régime* with Imperial, Victorian and older roots in British and Irish history.[36]

The revolutionary War of Independence concluded with the Treaty in December 1921. The Treaty, however, failed to deliver the separatist objective of an independent republic. Rather than the home rule granted by the Government of Ireland Act (1920), dominion rule and an Irish Free State became the basis for deadly civil war between Treatyites and anti-Treatyites. The Treatyites emerged victorious in 1923, and a period of peace and consolidation ensued in Ireland. The border of Northern Ireland and the Irish Free State was subsequently finalised in a tri-partite agreement between both parties and the British government in 1925.[37] The two modern Irelands which had emerged were counter-revolutionary regimes. The southern regime institutionalised a regime of 'Thermidor': the pro-Treaty side, the 'party of order', was pro-separatist but wished to consolidate the gains made in 1917–21.[38] The Northern Ireland regime, by contrast, was counter-revolutionary on the basis of defence of the British imperial state in Ireland; to further draw the analogy with Revolutionary France, we can consider Northern Ireland under the UUP a regime of 'Vendée'.[39]

plurality' voting for local government elections in 1921 and for parliamentary elections in 1929. See footnotes 46 and 48 below; see also Chap. 3 below.

[36] 'Too often, since every account must start somewhere, we see only the things which are new.' E. P. Thompson, *The Making*, p. 27.

[37] The most detailed examination of these events is by Paul Murray, *The Irish Boundary Commission*.

[38] Leon Trotsky utilised the French Revolution term 'Thermidor' to explicate the role of Stalin's communist regime. 'Thermidor' refers to the night in 1794 on which the Jacobins and Robespierre fell from power, but this revolt, against the Jacobins, was not in favour of the restoration of the *ancien régime*. 'Thermidor' therefore refers to counter-revolution within a revolution.

[39] The Vendée, a royalist rebellion in favour of the *ancien régime*, took place during the French Revolution in the western department of France; if we utilise an analogy of the French to the Irish revolutions, then the Northern Ireland state appears as a successful rebellion in

1.1.3   Institutionalising Loyalty

By the end of 1923, political violence in Ireland receded, and both admin-istrations in Ireland proceeded to consolidate their respective states. The Government of Ireland Act (1920) provided for excepted,[40] reserved[41] and devolved[42] powers. However, the economics of inter-war Northern Ireland never matched the optimistic model utilised as the basis for the 1920 Act. The unemployment fund for Northern Ireland was constituted on the basis of an unemployment rate at 7%.[43] Throughout the 1920s, unemployment averaged about double this figure, and consequently the Northern Ireland fund was soon insolvent. In 1925, however, the Colwyn committee reported that domestic services should be the first charge and the imperial contribution the last charge on the Northern Irish budget.[44] Furthermore, it was agreed that the Northern Ireland unemployment fund would be integrated into the UK fund in 1926. The agreement that year with Britain—and a further agreement which was negotiated in 1936[45]—allowed the regional administration to avoid falling into debt to meet the provision of unemployment benefit. The regional administration was also hampered financially by the decision to match British standards of social welfare.

Under Sir James Craig's direction in the 1920s, the UUP government decided to follow a policy of 'step-by-step' parity with British social wel-fare benefits. Yet this policy and the UUP administration created a pecu-

---

defence of the *ancien régime*. Similarly, the Irish Free State, Éire and Republic of Ireland all appear, by analogy, as regimes of Thermidor.

[40] Issues for which UK consensus was necessary (for example, the Crown, War, trade, money and the armed forces).

[41] Issues 'reserved' in the expectation of all-Ireland unity (for example, the Northern Ireland Supreme Court, postal services, deeds and certain important taxes).

[42] Issues which the Northern Ireland government and parliament had powers to legislate and administrate.

[43] Hazel Morrissey, 'Unemployment and the Northern Ireland State, 1919–39', in *The Other Crisis: Unemployment in Northern Ireland* ed. by Mike Morrissey (no place, no date of publications), p. 72; M. O. McCullagh, 'State Responses to Unemployment in Northern Ireland since 1922: A Sociological Analysis' (M. Sci. thesis, Queen's University Belfast, 1985), p. 75.

[44] Alvin Jackson, *Ireland, 1798–1998: Politics and War* (first ed., London, 1999), p. 349; Peter Martin, 'Social Policy and Social Change since 1914', in *Ulster since 1600: Politics, Economy and Society* ed. by Liam Kennedy and Philip Ollerenshaw (Oxford: Oxford University Press, 2013), pp. 308–24 (pp. 309–10).

[45] Alvin Jackson, *Ireland, 1798–1998*, p. 349.

liar regime in Northern Ireland. For example, to be eligible to vote at parliamentary elections and local elections and claim unemployment benefit, residency qualifications of three, and then seven, years were introduced during the inter-war period.[46] Such policies deliberately discriminated in favour of those already resident and were officially adopted to discourage southern Irish migration into Northern Ireland. But such policies 'politicised' the administration of the state in the province, and the distinctive welfare policy implemented by the UUP was matched by the severe security legislation applied in the region. The Civil Authorities (Special Powers) Act (Northern Ireland) differentiated the state in Northern Ireland from Britain.[47] The Special Powers Act, as it came to be known, was annually re-affirmed between 1922 and 1928. In 1928, it was passed for a five-year term; in 1933, it became a permanent piece of legislation. The existence of this distinctive and peculiar legislation became a major issue of contention for the civil rights movement in 1960s Northern Ireland.

In the mid-1920s, however, there was fear amongst the local Unionist elite that their position would be undermined by independent Unionists and socialists in Belfast. The Unionist maverick T. H. Sloan returned to Belfast in the mid-1920s, for example, whilst the NILP won three Northern Ireland parliament seats in Belfast at the second Northern Ireland parliamentary election in 1925. As a consequence, STV proportional representation was abolished for the next Northern Ireland parliamentary election.[48] The third Northern Ireland general election was held in May 1929 using simple plurality voting. The UUP won 37 seats, 16 unopposed; independent Unionists three seats; Nationalists 11 seats, six unopposed; and the NILP one seat. By 1929, the Northern Ireland state

---

[46] A three-year residency qualification to claim unemployment benefit was introduced in 1928. *Hansard N.I. (Commons)*, ix, 461 (20 March 1928); a seven-year residency qualification to claim unemployment benefit was introduced in 1934. *Ulster Year Book 1935*, p. 146. The residency qualification for unemployment benefit correlates with the three- and seven-year residency qualifications introduced for parliamentary and local government elections: for the Northern Ireland parliamentary franchise, see *Ulster Year Book 1929*, p. 219 and *Ulster Year Book 1935*, p. 271; for local election franchise, see *Ulster Year Book 1929*, p. 226, and *Ulster Year Book 1935*, p. 279.

[47] For in-depth discussion and analysis of how the Special Powers Act applied to the Belfast labour movement, see Chap. 4 below.

[48] STV proportional representation was introduced for Irish local elections in 1920; the new UUP government in Northern Ireland abolished this for local elections in 1922.

had been consolidated and was relatively peaceful. The UUP had achieved what appeared to be a political and electoral hegemony in Northern Ireland by the later 1920s. However, this was a 'dominance without hegemony' and at no point did Unionism feel secure within Northern Ireland.[49] The case studies below analyse the working-class politics of the Belfast labour movement. A central conclusion of the study will be how the UUP regime constructed politics and political culture as a moral economy of loyalty.

1.1.4   Northern Ireland and the 'Bones' of Loyalty

In the 1930s, economic problems in Northern Ireland were compounded by further political difficulties. The inter-war period was marked by over-capacity globally in both agriculture and industry. The same pressures which had contributed to war imperialism and competition between states for markets also drove the economic nationalism adopted in many parts of Europe during the inter-war years. Northern Ireland failed to re-capture its position as a leading centre of shipbuilding, engineering and textiles. These industries suffered from global competition, loss of market share, antiquated production techniques and loss of profitability. The 'rationalisation' of industries helped to cause temporary and structural unemployment as technology replaced labour.[50] This played a contributory role to the outdoor-relief riots of October 1932. The problems of industry in Northern Ireland were rooted in a difficult global economy, but political choices by the inter-war UUP administration also weakened local industry.[51] The resulting mass unemployment, both structural and temporary, effected sections of the working class which previously had

---

[49] The term is taken from an important piece of Indian Subaltern Studies, Ranajit Guha, *Dominance without Hegemony: History and Power in Colonial India* (Cambridge, MA: Harvard University Press, 1997).

[50] 'Rationalisation', technology, and industrial change lie outside the scope of the present short study. These topics will form the basis of future research and are especially relevant for the north of Ireland in 1900–50.

[51] The UUP administration had little control over 'reserved' or 'excepted' services. For example, Winston Churchill's decision to re-adopt the Gold Standard in 1925 made all British exports less competitive and the UUP was powerless to counteract this decision. However, the UUP administration also made relatively little effort to implement direct interventionist public sector policies. Rather, they preferred to use more 'traditional' methods such as public subsidies for private housing in the region.

been largely immune to such problems. For example, many shipbuilding and engineering workers, overwhelmingly male, found themselves unemployed as a result of problems within that industry, a situation exacerbated by the decision to shut the 'wee yard', Workman and Clark, in 1935. The textile industry, which had a largely female workforce, was similarly effected by economic problems during the inter-war period. Economic dislocation, a result of war, revolution and partition, was worsened by the Anglo-Irish trade war between 1932 and 1938. It was only as the decade came to a close that the re-armament boom in Britain started to have some limited impact on Northern Ireland.[52]

The UUP administration faced weak electoral opposition during this period and this accounts for why the regime appeared to be hegemonic.[53] The most significant reason for this UUP dominance was the explicit control exercised by the party. The political culture of Northern Ireland was rooted in Victorian and Edwardian conceptions of liberal democracy, whereby rights were linked to property as opposed to the individual. This was allied to a strong majoritarianism, that democracy should prioritise the interests of the majority over the rights of minorities. The result was a peculiar regime of, essentially, plebiscitary democracy. There were also, however, some areas of reform. Housing and social welfare were subject to serious reform. The Loans Guarantee Act managed to keep some shipbuilding jobs in Northern Ireland.[54] Agricultural marketing boards were organised which marketed, produced and standardised products from Northern Irish farms being sold domestically and internationally.[55]

Northern Ireland by the end of 1932 had hit a severe trough of unemployment. The refusal of the local Poor Law Guardians to grant sufficient Outdoor Relief led to riots by both working-class Protestants and Catholics

---

[52] See Boyd Black, 'A Triumph of Voluntarism?'; C. J. V. Loughlin, 'Pro-Hitler or Anti-Management? War on the Industrial Front, Belfast, October 1942', in *Locked Out: A Century of Irish Working-Class Life* ed. by David Convery (Dublin Academic Press, 2013), pp. 125–39.

[53] 'Hegemony' is here utilised as dominance without coercion. See Ranajit Guha, *Dominance without Hegemony*.

[54] See Christopher Norton, 'Creating Jobs, Manufacturing Unity: Ulster Unionism and Mass Unemployment, 1922–34', *Contemporary British History*, 15, No. 2 (June 2001), 1–14.

[55] Patrick Buckland, *The Factory of Grievances: Devolved Government in Northern Ireland, 1921–39* (Dublin: Gill and Macmillan, 1979).

in October 1932. This was the context for the fourth Northern Ireland general election in November 1933. The House of Commons met in the newly opened Stormont building. The UUP won 36 MPs, an impressive 27 unopposed; independent Unionists three MPs; Nationalists nine MPs, six unopposed; the NILP two MPs; and Fianna Fáil and Sinn Féin, one MP each. State power was further consolidated by the passage of the Special Powers Act as a permanent piece of legislation in 1933. In these years of economic and political problems, the UUP engaged in explicitly sectarian rhetoric.[56] The bombast of the UUP elite, however, contradicted section five of the Government of Ireland Act (1920), which prohibited religious endorsement or discrimination. Some analysts have further claimed that Northern Ireland was, in fact, a Protestant state.[57] In contrast to analyses which prioritise religion, the analysis presented below, on Labour's politics of disloyalty in Belfast, will examine how the intra–Northern Ireland political culture created by the UUP constituted a moral economy of loyalty. The Belfast riots of 1935, the adoption of a new constitution in southern Ireland and the ending of the 'Economic War' between Britain and Ireland form the context for the last Northern Ireland general election for the era under consideration.

The fifth Northern Ireland general election took place on 9 February 1938. The UUP gained 39 seats (including 14 unopposed returns), independent Unionists three seats, Nationalists eight seats (six unopposed) and NILP one seat (elected unopposed) plus independent Labour, one seat.[58] Northern Ireland by 1939 exhibited all the problems associated in Britain with 'distressed areas', such as parts of Scotland, Wales and northern England. These were primarily problems of industrial decline, decreasing profitability and consequent mass unemployment. However, despite these far-from-auspicious circumstances, the Northern Ireland state had been successfully created and consolidated. Measures of industrial reform, welfare change and educational reorganisation had been instituted.

---

[56] Sir Basil Brooke was reported as stating on 12 July 1933 that 'he would appeal to Loyalists therefore, wherever possible, to employ good Protestant lads and lassies'. Quoted in Michael Farrell, *Northern Ireland: The Orange State* (second ed., London: Pluto Press, 1980), p. 90; Sir James Craig remarked in the Northern Ireland House of Commons in May 1934: 'all I boast is that we are a Protestant parliament and a Protestant state'. *Hansard Northern Ireland (Commons)*, xvi, 1095 (24 April 1934).

[57] See Chaps. 2 and 4 below.

[58] Jack Beattie maintained his seat in 1938 but had been expelled from the NILP in 1934 for refusing to move the writ for the late Joe Devlin's seat in Belfast Central division.

Therefore, alongside acts of Unionist misgovernment—such as the aboli-tion of STV for local elections and politically discriminatory policies—must be set the successful creation of the Northern Ireland state.

1.2 SECTION II: HISTORY, LABOUR AND NORTHERN IRELAND, 1921–39

1.2.1 The Peculiarities of Northern Ireland

The second section of the introduction surveys the historiographical knowledge on labour in inter-war Northern Ireland. This material is com-plex because of the contribution of both British and Irish history. Furthermore, analysis of Belfast, Northern Ireland and the moral econ-omy of loyalty should be placed within four nations, imperial and global historical contexts. However, within this work, the priority for analysis is intra–Northern Ireland politics, in general, and Belfast politics, in particu-lar. It has therefore not been possible to address the intra–British Isles, transnational or global contexts of the moral economy of loyalty; these areas await future research and publication.

J. H. Whyte, writing in 1990, suggested that there were four general analytical frameworks with which to understand Northern Ireland: the traditional Nationalist interpretation, the traditional Unionist interpreta-tion, the Marxist interpretation, and the ethnic-conflict zone interpreta-tion.[59] These paradigmatic interpretations should be supplemented by developments in Irish Studies[60] and socio-economic,[61] gender,[62] post-

---

[59] J. H. Whyte, *Interpreting Northern Ireland* (Oxford: Clarendon Press, 1990).

[60] *Ireland beyond Boundaries: Mapping Irish Studies in the Twenty-First Century* ed. by Liam Harte and Yvonne Whelan (London; Ann Arbor, MI: Pluto Press, 2007); Dominic Bryan, *Orange Parades: The Politics of Ritual, Tradition and Control* (London: Pluto Press, 2000).

[61] *An Economic History of Ulster, 1820–1939* ed. by Liam Kennedy and Philip Ollerenshaw (Manchester: Manchester University Press, 1985); *Ulster since 1600: Politics, Economy and Society* ed. by Liam Kennedy and Philip Ollerenshaw.

[62] Mary McAuliffe, *Palgrave Advances in Irish History* ed. by Mary McAuliffe, Katherine O'Donnell and Leeann Lane (Basingstoke and New York: Palgrave Macmillan, 2009), pp. 191–221; Sean Brady, 'Why Examine Men, Masculinities and Religion in Northern Ireland?', in *Masculinities and Religious Change in Twentieth-Century Britain* ed. by Lucy Delap and Sue Morgan (Basingstoke, 2013), pp. 218–51; Maria Luddy, 'Gender and Irish History', in *The Oxford Handbook of Modern Irish History* ed. by Alvin Jackson (Oxford: Oxford University Press, 2014), pp. 193–213; J. G. V. McGaughey, *Ulster's Men*.

colonial,[63] and new revolutionary[64] studies approaches to twentieth-century Irish history. The traditional Nationalist interpretation views Ireland as one nation and attributes the division of the island to British interest. The 'revisionist controversy', particularly acute in the late 1980s and 1990s, largely focused on the legacy of the Nationalist interpretation within historical analysis.[65]

The traditional Unionist analysis, by contrast, interprets Ireland as divided between two nations: one British and predominantly Protestant, the other Irish and predominantly Catholic. As a consequence, Ulster Unionist interpretations attribute conflict in Ireland to Nationalists' failure to accept self-determination for the British community on the island.[66] The credibility of the Unionist position has been undermined by the record of sectarian discrimination by the devolved Northern Ireland administration between 1921 and 1972.[67] There has also been important

[63] This work begins with the seminal book by David Cairns and Shaun Richards, *Writing Ireland: Colonialism, Nationalism and Culture* (Manchester: Manchester University Press, 1988); see also *Ireland and Postcolonial Theory* ed. by Clare Carroll and Patricia King (Notre Dame, IN: University of Notre Dame Press, 2003); Joe Cleary, 'Misplaced Ideas? Locating and Dislocating Ireland in Colonial and Postcolonial Studies', in *Marxism, Modernity and Postcolonial Studies* ed. by Crystal Bartolovich and Neil Lazarus (Cambridge: Cambridge University Press, 2002), pp. 101–24; Colin Graham, *Deconstructing Ireland: Identity, Theory, Culture* (Edinburgh: Edinburgh University Press, 2001); *Irish and Postcolonial Writing: History, Theory and Practice* ed. by Glenn Hooper and Colin Graham (Houndmills: Palgrave Macmillan, 2002); David Lloyd, *Ireland after History* (Cork: Cork University Press, 1998).

[64] See, for example, the work of Timothy Bowman, *Carson's Army: The Ulster Volunteer Force, 1910–22* (Manchester: Manchester University Press, 2007); Marie Coleman, *The Irish Revolution*; David Fitzpatrick, *The Two Irelands, 1921–39* (Oxford: Oxford University Press, 1998); Peter Harte, *The IRA and Its Enemies: Violence and Community in Cork* (Oxford: Clarendon Press, 1998); Peter Harte, *The IRA at War* (Oxford: Oxford University Press, 2003); and Fearghal McGarry, *The Rising: Easter 1916* (Oxford: Oxford University Press, 2010).

[65] See *The Making of Modern Irish History: Revisionism and the Revisionist Controversy* ed. by D. G. Boyce and Alan O'Day (London: Routledge, 1996); and *Interpreting Irish History: The Debate on Historical Revisionism, 1938–1994* ed. by Ciaran Brady (Dublin: Irish Academic Press, 1994).

[66] J. H. Whyte, *Interpreting Northern Ireland*, p. 146.

[67] See Paul Bew, Peter Gibbon, and Henry Patterson, *Northern Ireland 1921–2001: Political Forces and Social Classes* (revised ed., London: Serif, 2002); Patrick Buckland, *The Factory of Grievance*; Idem, *James Craig, Lord Craigavon* (Dublin: Gill & Macmillan, 1980); Patrick Buckland, 'A Protestant State: Unionists in Government, 1921–39', in *Defenders of*

work on the history and creation of a specific Ulster Unionist identity.[68] This material has been supplemented by work on women's Unionism and Protestant Unionist masculinities.[69] For the case studies in this book, however, the politics of nationalism, discrimination and identity are key issues of intra–Northern Ireland relations.[70]

Marxist interpretation in Ireland has been primarily associated with James Connolly's legacy, and the reception of Connolly's thought is the story of Irish Marxism.[71] Marxist analyses (influenced by the Connollyite tradition), such as that of Michael Farrell, sympathise with the Nationalist interpretation.[72] Marxists in the 1960s, however, became politically divided in their analysis of Northern Ireland. For example, Paul Bew, Peter Gibbon and Henry Patterson (hereafter referred to as Bew *et al.*) analysed the history of Northern Ireland in a way that was more sympathetic to the Unionist position.[73] What unites Bew *et al.* and Connollyite analyses is their use of 'integralist class analysis'.[74] Examples are the Connollyite argument for Britain's strategic and imperialist economic interest in setting up Northern Ireland[75] and, further, the Bew *et al.* aim of seeking to understand the pan-Protestant Unionist bloc through a class framework.[76] The Marxist approach has also had significant wider influence due to the adoption of terms such as 'class', 'hegemony' and 'uneven development' in wider discourse.

the Union: A Survey of British and Irish Unionism since 1801 ed. by D. G. Boyce and Alan O'Day (London: Routledge, 2001), pp. 211–26; Michael Farrell, *Northern Ireland.*

[68] Henry Patterson, 'Unionism, 1921–72', in *The Oxford Handbook of Modern Irish History*, pp. 692–710.

[69] J. G. V. McGahey, *Ulster's Men; The Minutes of the Ulster Women's Unionist Council and Executive Committee, 1911–1940* ed. by Diane Urquhart (Dublin: Women's History Project in association with Irish Manuscripts Commission, 2001); Diane Urquhart, *Women in Ulster Politics, 1890–1940: A History Not Yet Told* (Dublin: Irish Academic Press, 2000).

[70] Chapter 2 below concentrates on investigating the politics of nationality, sectarianism and the labour movement in Belfast.

[71] C. J. V. Loughlin, 'Representing Labour', p. 68.

[72] Michael Farrell, *Northern Ireland.*

[73] Paul Bew, Peter Gibbon, and Henry Patterson, *Northern Ireland 1921–2001.*

[74] Kolakowski described Marxism as an 'integral theory of mankind'. See Leszek Kolakowski, *Main Currents of Marxism: Its Rise, Growth and Dissolution*, 3 vols. (Oxford: Clarendon Press, 1978), I: *The Founders*, p. 6. The phrase 'integralist class analysis' is coined in section three of C. J. V. Loughlin, 'Representing Labour'.

[75] Michael Farrell, *Northern Ireland*, pp. 325–6.

[76] Paul Bew, Peter Gibbon, and Henry Patterson, *Northern Ireland: 1921–2001*, pp. 18–19.

Sympathetic to developments in Marxist analysis is the ethnic-conflict zone interpretation, which developed out of social scientific perspectives on Northern Ireland. The best known example is Brendan O'Leary and John McGarry's analysis, *The Politics of Antagonism*. They argued that the Unionist regime in Northern Ireland between 1920 and 1972 was one of 'hegemonic control', which they defined as 'a system of ethnic domination, in which the power-holders make revolt by the controlled ethnic group(s) unworkable'. McGarry and O'Leary claimed 'hegemonic control' was an accurate description because of the evidence of territorial, constitutional, electoral, coercive, legal, economic and administrative control by the Ulster Unionist administration. This bleak assessment, however, argued that 'hegemonic control is entirely compatible with the Westminster model of representative government'.[77] It became clear during the case studies below that the term 'hegemony' had been misused in previous studies on Northern Ireland. The UUP administration of Northern Ireland created a dominance in the region, but it lacked democratic legitimacy and hegemony. What about the role of sectarianism, Christian-based, ethno-national conflict and violence?[78]

There is a tendency to see sectarian conflict in Northern Ireland as inevitable. Alvin Jackson, for example, in an important survey of Irish history, claimed that northern Catholics were always likely to suffer because of the 'endemic' sectarianism in the region.[79] Michael Farrell has argued that religious discrimination in employment gave 'Protestants a small but real advantage', resulting in the creation of a 'Protestant "aristocracy of labour"'.[80] He claimed that Labour was unable to capitalise on the working-class unity demonstrated in Belfast in 1932 because it came 'up against the question of discrimination and Protestant privilege'. For Farrell, the UUP, even when it sought to make tactical concessions to

---

[77] Brendan O'Leary and John McGarry, *The Politics of Antagonism: Understanding Northern Ireland* (second ed., London: Athlone Press, 1997), p. 371 (pp. 111–33 and p. 134).

[78] Here defined as Christian-based ethno-national conflict. See Chaps. 2 and 4 below.

[79] Alvin Jackson, *Ireland 1798–1998*, p. 345.

[80] Michael Farrell, *Northern Ireland*, p. 11; the analysis presented below does not analyse the issue of the 'aristocracy of labour' or the political import of this term. It should, however, be noted that Marx describes, in a later section of the first volume of *Capital*, the best paid section of the working class as an 'aristocracy'. See Karl Marx, *Capital: A Critique of Political Economy* trans. by Ben Fowkes, 3 vols. (London: Penguin Books in association with New Left Review, 1976), I, p. 822.

Nationalists, was 'shackled to Protestant supremacy'.[81] Bew *et al.* have argued that it is not obvious that the Protestant working class was bought off with privileges any more than Catholics were radicalised by them.[82] For these authors, policing and security were used, essentially, as a form of clientelism for those who were 'loyal', Protestants and Unionists.[83] When Northern Ireland was set up, according to Bew *et al.*, the Ulster Unionist elite was forced to concede a portion of its power to working-class Protestants.[84] The sectarian patronage offered by the 'populists' in the state administration (led by James Craig, J. M. Andrews and Dawson Bates) resulted in 'the continued split between the Protestant and Catholic working class'.[85] Bew *et al.* agree that Britain played an important role, but they do not stress the role of imperialism as other authors have.[86] The case studies, presented below, investigate how the Belfast labour movement dealt with and explained the issue of division in the province.

1.2.2   Loyalty and Sectarianism

Historians have emphasised the success and extent of the control established by the UUP after partition. K. T. Hoppen has written that, despite the violent conditions in 1920–22, 'Unionism … had little difficulty in maintaining that pan-class alliance'.[87] There is further consensus that it was unlikely that the Northern Ireland state could have been vibrant and successful.[88] However, Brian Barton has claimed that 'there were some grounds for optimism' that a stable Ulster Unionist government would be broader than just a 'Protestant ascendancy'.[89] It seemed possible that

---

[81] Michael Farrell, *Northern Ireland*, p. 327.

[82] Paul Bew, Peter Gibbon, and Henry Patterson, 'Some Aspects of Nationalism and Socialism in Ireland: 1968–78', in *Ireland: Divided Nation, Divided Class* ed. by Austen Morgan and Bob Purdie (London: Ink Links, 1980), pp. 152–72 (pp. 157–8).

[83] Paul Bew, Peter Gibbon, and Henry Patterson, *Northern Ireland 1921–2001*, pp. 32–3.

[84] Ibid., pp. 18–19.

[85] Ibid., p. 60.

[86] Michael Farrell, *Northern Ireland*, pp. 325–6; Paul Stewart, 'The Jerrybuilders: Bew, Gibbon and Patterson—The Protestant Working Class and the Northern Irish State', in *Ireland's Histories: Aspects of State, Society and Ideology* ed. by Seán Hutton and Paul Stewart (London, 1991), pp. 177–202 (p. 186).

[87] K. T. Hoppen, *Ireland since 1800: Conflict and Conformity* (second ed., London: Longman, 1999), p. 210.

[88] Patrick Buckland, 'A Protestant State', p. 216; Michael Farrell, *Northern Ireland*, p. 332.

[89] Brian Barton, 'Northern Ireland, 1921–5', in *A New History of Ireland* (Oxford: Clarendon Press, 2003), VII: *Ireland 1921–84*, ed. by J. R. Hill, pp. 161–98 (pp. 162–3).

social and economic issues could come to the fore in the new polity of Northern Ireland.[90] Such hopes were dashed, however, because the 'circumstances of Northern Ireland's birth permanently distorted its political structures'.[91] Sectarian tension, the Unionist siege mentality, an antagonistic southern neighbour, and fear of Britain pulling out shaped the state. Patrick Buckland's analysis is, generally, even more negative than Barton's. Whilst Craig was militarily successful in establishing the state, he failed to rise to the challenge of peacetime leadership.[92] Furthermore, for Buckland, it was inevitable that Northern Ireland would be politically dysfunctional because Catholics and Protestants managed to live in relative peace through mutual isolation.[93] This was compounded by the localism and patronage of Ulster Unionist 'political culture' and the conflicting pressures on devolved government by local authorities, the Imperial British government, and an irredentist southern neighbour.[94] According to Buckland, only a heroic prime minister could have dealt with the problems facing the state, and ultimately there were too many obstacles to the development of a healthy political culture in Northern Ireland.[95]

The extent of misgovernment practised by the UUP in the inter-war period has been the subject of much debate,[96] but it is accepted that discriminatory practice was widespread. Much of this debate has also focused on Northern Ireland in the post–Second World War period. Buckland has accepted that there was a 'majority dictatorship' but argued that it should not be exaggerated.[97] For Buckland, Craig abolished proportional representation for local elections in 1922 as a sop to his ministerial colleagues

---

[90] Ibid.
[91] Ibid., p. 171.
[92] Patrick Buckland, *James Craig*, p. 89.
[93] Idem, 'A Protestant State', pp. 216–17.
[94] Ibid., pp. 218–20.
[95] Patrick Buckland, *James Craig*, p. 125.
[96] The primary sources on this issue will be examined below, but serious analysis of the issue begins with the Cameron Report (1969); the issues raised by this report were the subject of major debate on the issue during the 1970s and 1980s conducted by sociologists. See Conflict Archive on the Internet (CAIN), 'Discrimination-Details of Source Material' <http://cain.ulst.ac.uk/issues/discrimination/soc.htm> [accessed 1 May 2017]; see also J Whyte John Whyte, 'How much Discrimination was there under the Unionist regime, 1921–68?' (Manchester: Manchester University Press, 1983) <cain.ulst.ac.uk/issues/discrimination/whyte.htm> [accessed 1 May 2017]; John O'Brien, *Discrimination in Northern Ireland, 1920–39: Myth or Reality?* (Cambridge, 2010).
[97] Patrick Buckland, 'A Protestant State', p. 211.

and was unaware of the potential long-term impact on the development of Northern Ireland.[98] In 1928, Craig abolished proportional representation for Northern Ireland parliamentary elections.[99] D. G. Pringle claimed that the change in voting procedures for parliament was a deliberate and calculated political manoeuvre.[100] Abolition was carried out 'to establish greater control of the Protestant vote, rather than to discriminate against Catholics'.[101] Pringle highlights evidence that when the boundaries for parliamentary elections were redrawn they were not redrawn to systematically disenfranchise Catholics.[102] Rather, the aim was to regain seats lost by the UUP, primarily in Belfast, to independent Unionists and the NILP.[103] Barton and Farrell emphasised that the purpose of this act of Unionist misgovernment was both to discriminate and to maintain electoral support for the UUP.[104]

The culpability of the Ulster Unionist elite for encouraging sectarian practises has also generated debate. Marxist orthodoxy on Northern Ireland argues that the rhetoric deployed by the Unionist elite was a significant cause of sectarianism.[105] This has been challenged by Ronnie Munck and Bill Rolston, who argued that sectarianism could not be set off at whim by the UUP.[106] Christopher Norton has demonstrated a nuanced orthodox Marxist interpretation.[107] He described the employers' ineffective reaction to the 1920 shipyard expulsions as 'at best an indifference for the wellbeing of their employees'.[108] Patrick Buckland, however, has stated that 'it is a moot question as to how far employers and political and reli-

---

[98] Patrick Buckland, *James Craig*, p. 82.

[99] Ibid., p. 111.

[100] D. G. Pringle, 'Electoral Systems and Political Manipulation: A Case Study of Northern Ireland in the 1920s', *The Economic and Social Review*, 11, No. 11 (1980), 187–205 (188).

[101] Ibid.

[102] Ibid., p. 199.

[103] Ibid., pp. 200–1.

[104] Brian Barton, 'Northern Ireland, 1921–5', pp. 192–4; Michael Farrell, *Northern Ireland*, pp. 83–5.

[105] Mike Milotte, *Communism in Modern Ireland: The Pursuit of the Workers' Republic since 1916* (Dublin: Gill & Macmillan, 1984), p. 123; see also Henry Patterson, *Class Conflict and Sectarianism*.

[106] Ronnie Munck and Bill Rolston, *Belfast in the Thirties: An Oral History* (Belfast: Blackstaff Press, 1987), pp. 8–9.

[107] Christopher Norton, 'Worker Response to the 1920 Belfast Shipyard Expulsions', *Études-Irelandaises* (Spring 1996), 153–63.

[108] Ibid., p. 155.

gious leaders deliberately and consistently exploited the sectarian question to keep workers docile and malleable'.[109] It is undeniable that the Ulster Unionist leadership utilised sectarian rhetoric.[110] This is demonstrated in Sir James Craig and Sir Edward Carson's comments in the summer of 1920 about 'Bolshevik-Sinn Feiners' which precipitated sectarian expulsions in the workplace.[111] Similar explicit sectarian comments were made by Sir Basil Brooke in 1933 and Lord Craigavon in 1934.[112] The consequence and reality of discrimination are also demonstrable.[113] Yet there were a number of safeguards implemented in the Government of Ireland Act (1920) to prevent religious discrimination. For example, STV proportional representation, for both local and parliamentary elections, was to ensure the representation of minorities, whilst section five of the Government of Ireland Act also expressly forbade religious endorsement or prohibition. Therefore, we are left with an issue in history and historical knowledge: was Northern Ireland a Protestant regime? The politics of loyalty and disloyalty was the means by which discrimination was conducted: all those considered 'disloyal' were liable to suffer victimisation, abuse, conflict and at times even explicit violence. The moral economy of loyalty expresses the 'rules of the game' constructed by the UUP in 1921–39.[114] The politics of disloyalty is how the peculiar regime in Northern Ireland was able to construct a state, arguably, within the bounds of the Government of Ireland Act. Furthermore, the politics of loyalty constructed by the UUP was a 'dominance without hegemony'.[115]

1.2.3   Labour and Working-Class Politics in Belfast

Labour history in Irish academia is a relatively recent phenomenon but in 1974 was given institutional form with the foundation of the Irish Labour History Society and the launch of the society's journal, *Saothar*. Before this, most inquiry into labour history was carried out by politically motivated activists, who were primarily left-wing.[116] The important work of

---

[109] Patrick Buckland, 'A Protestant State', p. 223.

[110] See Chap. 2 below.

[111] Michael Farrell, *Northern Ireland*, p. 27.

[112] See footnote 56 above.

[113] See footnote 96 above.

[114] The title of the famous 1939 Jean Renoir film, *La Règle du Jeu* (translated as *The Rules of the Game*).

[115] See footnotes 49 and 53 above.

[116] Fintan Lane, 'Envisaging Labour History: Some Reflections on Irish Historiography and the Working Class', in *Essays in Irish labour History: A Festschrift for Elizabeth and John*

scholars such as J. W. Boyle, Emmet O'Connor and Boyd Black is today being matched by a new generation of scholarship.[117] O'Connor has described Labour in Ireland as shaped by a 'colonial legacy'.[118] He has further contended that the main area of conflict for the labour movement in the north of Ireland was between competing Labour and Loyalist identities rather than conflict between Protestants and Catholics.[119] O'Connor's position can be contrasted with Boyd Black's thesis about the development of a British industrial relations system in the north of Ireland.[120] Norton, however, has queried O'Connor's description of the Northern Ireland trade unions as led by anti-UUP elements but made up of Loyalist rank and file members.[121] Norton states that those who took part in the 1920 expulsions, for example, were primarily semi- and unskilled workers.[122] For him, the economic vulnerability of this layer of working-class Protestants—not their 'privileges'—caused their strong sectarian consciousness. This controversy in labour history is a continuation of the wider debates on the Northern Ireland question noted above.

There has been significant debate on cross-community politics and sectarianism in the north of Ireland. Debate on cross-community working-class politics has hinged on its feasibility in Northern Ireland.[123] J. W. Boyle claimed they were inherently linked: when sectarianism was in the ascendant, then non-sectarian politics was in decline, and vice versa.[124]

W. Boyle ed. by Francis Devine, Fintan Lane, and Niámh Puirséil (Dublin: Irish Academic Press, 2008), pp. 9–25 (p. 11).

[117] Emmet O'Connor, *A Labour History of Ireland, 1824–1960* (Dublin: Gill & Macmillan, 1992); Emmet O'Connor, *A Labour History of Ireland, 1824–2000* (second revised ed., Dublin: University College Dublin Press, 2011); Boyd Black, 'Reassessing Irish Industrial Relations and Labour History: The North-East of Ireland up to 1921', *Historical Studies in Industrial Relations*, 14 (Autumn 2002), 45–97; Boyd Black, 'A Triumph of Voluntarism?'; Michael Pierse, *Writing Ireland's Working Class, A Cambridge History of Irish Working-Class Writing* ed. by Michael Pierse.

[118] Emmet O'Connor, 'Labour and Politics: Colonisation and Mental Colonisation', in *Politics and the Irish Working Class, 1830–1945* ed. by Donal Ó Drisceoil and Fintan Lane (Basingstoke: Palgrave Macmillan, 2005), pp. 27–43.

[119] Emmet O'Connor, *A Labour History of Ireland, 1824–2000*, p. 188.

[120] Boyd Black, 'Reassessing Irish Industrial Relations'.

[121] Christopher Norton, '1920 Belfast Shipyard Expulsions', p. 154.

[122] Ibid., p. 155.

[123] Emmet O'Connor, 'A Historiography of Irish Labour', pp. 29–30.

[124] Martin Maguire, '"Remembering Who We Are": Identity and Class in Protestant Dublin and Belfast, 1868–1905', in *Essays in Irish Labour History: A Festschrift for Elizabeth and John W. Boyle*, pp. 49–64.

Boyle's analysis of the Independent Orange Order (IOO) in the first decade of the twentieth century argued that this signalled the decline of sectarian politics, for a period, and the consequent ascendancy of non-sectarian politics.[125] Henry Patterson, in contrast, argued that the IOO represented class consciousness in 'sectarian terms'.[126] Patterson's analysis has been described as one which interprets 'sectarianism as conjunctional rather than endemic'.[127] Furthermore, Munck and Rolston have argued that sectarian and non-sectarian politics could coexist and that they were not necessarily dependent on each other.[128] Graham Walker and John Lynch have stressed the material basis of the origins of sectarian rivalry among Catholic migrants who moved to Belfast during its industrial expansion in the nineteenth century.[129]

It is also linked to the debate about the 'failure' of the labour movement in the inter-war period and after. The academic consensus is that Labour was a political failure. In an unsympathetic analysis, Rumpf and Hepburn concluded that 'the NILP's limited degree of success has been achieved by effective manipulation of this balance [of religious demography in each constituency], by being different things to different men, or by coming forward on a compromise platform, and not by uninhibited and uncluttered advocacy of social and economic reforms'.[130] However, Christopher Norton and Aaron Edwards, while accepting the electoral failure of Labour in Northern Ireland, have argued that Labour's record was not one of unmitigated catastrophe. Norton has claimed that the mere existence of an alternative political tradition, as exemplified by the Northern Ireland labour movement, throughout the inter-war period was an achievement given the negative circumstance of a partitioned state.[131] Aaron Edwards has similarly described the inter-war labour movement as

---

[125] Ibid.

[126] Henry Patterson, *Class Conflict and Sectarianism*, p. 65.

[127] Emmet O'Connor, 'A Historiography of Irish Labour', *Labour History Review*, 40, part one (1995), 21–34 (27).

[128] Ronnie Munck and Bill Rolston, *Belfast in the Thirties*, p. 9.

[129] John Lynch, *A Tale of Three Cities: Comparative Studies in Working-Class Life* (Basingstoke: Palgrave Macmillan, 1998), p. 174; Graham Walker, *The Politics of Frustration: Harry Midgley and the Failure of Labour in Northern Ireland* (Manchester: Manchester University Press, 1985), p. 2.

[130] Erhard Rumpf and A. C. Hepburn, *Nationalism and Socialism in Twentieth-Century Ireland* (Liverpool: Liverpool University Press, 1977), pp. 195–6.

[131] Christopher Norton, 'The Left in Northern Ireland 1921–32', p. 15.

reasonably successful.[132] The present book concurs with the claim of Norton and Edwards: Labour was an electoral failure in Northern Ireland, but the political culture constructed in the region essentially guaranteed Labour's political impotence.

One event during the inter-war period in Belfast has caused more historical controversy than any other: the Outdoor Relief riots of October 1932. These riots occurred when working-class Protestants and Catholics agitated successfully for better rates of outdoor relief for the unemployed. In the immediate aftermath of these events, communists in Ireland described it as evidence of the disintegration of sectarian politics in Northern Ireland.[133] Subsequently, Munck and Rolston claim, a myth developed which posited that sectarian manipulation, by the leadership of the UUP, prevented the emergence of cross-community working-class politics.[134] Mike Milotte challenged this view, arguing that as important for the failure of non-sectarian politics was the defeat of the National Union of Railwaymen strike in Northern Ireland in 1933.[135] He attributed the riots of 1932 to the sheer desperation of the unemployed rather than any conscious adoption of all-Ireland politics by the Protestant lower classes.[136] Hoppen and Jackson, like most historians, have interpreted this event as the exception that proves the dominance of sectarian politics.[137] However, the importance of the debate is that the Outdoor Relief riots were an example of successful cross-community class politics in inter-war Northern Ireland.

The inter-war Belfast labour movement remains relatively under-researched. Henry Patterson and Austen Morgan have produced authoritative studies of the Belfast labour movement between 1880 and 1920.[138] Mike Milotte's study of communist politics in Ireland remains important but reflects a strong anti-Stalinist bias.[139] Graham Walker's biography of

[132] Aaron Edwards, *A History of the Northern Ireland Labour Party: Democratic Socialism and Sectarianism* (Manchester: Manchester University Press, 2009), p. 24.

[133] Ronnie Munck and Bill Rolston, *Belfast in the Thirties*, p. 7.

[134] Ibid., p. 9.

[135] Mike Milotte, *Communism in Modern Ireland*, p. 140.

[136] Ibid., p. 135.

[137] To cite just two examples, K. T. Hoppen, *Ireland since 1800*, p. 208; Alvin Jackson, *Ireland 1798–1998*, pp. 349–50.

[138] Austen Morgan, *Labour and Partition*; Henry Patterson, *Class Conflict and Sectarianism*.

[139] Mike Milotte, 'Communist Politics in Ireland, 1916–45' (PhD thesis, Queen's University Belfast, 1977); Idem, *Communism in Modern Ireland*.

Harry Midgley remains the definitive biography of the inter-war Belfast labour leader.[140] But, concentrating on one individual, Walker was unable to delineate the wider context or broader movement. Aaron Edwards's recent book on the NILP is authoritative on the post–Second World War development of the party.[141] But, owing to the lack of sources for the period, Edwards's chapter on the inter-war development of the NILP left a significant gap in historical understanding.[142] Seán Byers's recent book on Seán Murray also illuminated some aspects of the inter-war Northern Ireland labour movement, whilst Adrian Grant has offered important theses related to Republican socialism and the history of the Irish working class.[143] The present book therefore addresses the gap left in historical knowledge about the inter-war Belfast labour movement.

1.2.4   Labour and the Politics of Disloyalty in Belfast, 1921–39: The Moral Economy of Loyalty

A central conclusion of the case studies below is on the constitution of the 'rules of the game' of politics in inter-war Northern Ireland. The political culture of the region was dominated by the couplet loyalty/disloyalty: Belfast, for example, was dominated by a politics and linguistics of loyalty. Furthermore, the politics of popular mobilisation point to a notion of legitimation of political conflict and violence in the era under consideration: Belfast and Northern Ireland, the case studies suggest, was a moral economy of loyalty. The moral economy of loyalty was the 'notion of legitimation'[144] underpinning the Northern Ireland state in 1921–39. The term 'moral economy' was used by E. P. Thompson to designate a 'notion of legitimation ... [that men and women] were informed by the belief that they were defending traditional rights or customs; and, in general, that they were supported by the wider consensus of the community'.[145] He

[140] Graham Walker, 'Harry Midgley: A Study in Ulster Political Biography' (PhD thesis, Manchester University, 1983); Idem, *The Politics of Frustration*.

[141] Aaron Edwards, 'Labour Politics and Sectarianism: Interpreting the Political Fortunes of the Northern Ireland Labour Party, 1945–75' (PhD thesis, Queen's University Belfast, 2006); Idem, *A History of the Northern Ireland Labour Party*.

[142] Ibid., pp. 7–29.

[143] Seán Byers, 'Seán Murray's Political Apprenticeship: The Making of an Irish Republican Bolshevik', *Saothar*, 37 (2012), 41–55; Seán Byers, Seán Murray: *Marxist-Leninist and Irish Socialist Republican* (Dublin, 2015); Adrian Grant, *Irish Socialist Republicanism, 1909–36* (Dublin: Four Courts Press, 2012).

[144] E. P. Thompson, 'The Moral Economy of the English Crowd in the Eighteenth Century', in *Customs in Common* (London: Penguin Books, 1993), pp. 185–258 (p. 188).

[145] Ibid.

further claimed that 'moral economy' was how 'many "economic" relations are regulated according to non-monetary norms' in peasant and early modern communities.[146] The word 'loyalty' is used by the present author in the sense applied by D.W. Miller in his influential study *Queen's Rebels*.[147] Miller described Victorian and Edwardian Ulster unionism as motivated by 'loyalty', something 'quite different from nationality'. He continued, 'loyalty is a moral principle translated from the realm of personal relationships into politics…it carries the connotations of lawfulness, which Protestants understood to be what distinguished them from Catholic fellow-countrymen'.[148] In particular, the moral economy of loyalty will be demonstrated as a conclusion of the case studies below.

The moral economy of loyalty was the politics of democratic counter-revolution, or a democratised *ancien régime*.[149] The period of 1921–39, in Northern Ireland, involved old contexts (such as the early modern history of Ulster; religious division), a new mass tradition of loyalty and a new context of the regionalisation of the Irish question in British politics. The phrase and term also link to the wider historiography of popular politics, militarism, mobilisation and the history of social movements in the past 500 years. For example, the role of moral economy and rural and urban politics in Ireland in 1760–1840 but also the historiography of the Irish revolution.[150] The new social interpretation of the Irish revolution involves the social, economic and political investigation of the politics of popular mobilisation and mass-producing traditions. Similarly, the case studies below contribute to four nations' history, transnational history, imperial history and European comparative political sociology. Unfortunately, it has not been possible in a short book such as this one to investigate thoroughly the inter- and trans-national links of the moral economy of loyalty. These investigations will await future research, but for the present:

Hic Rhodus, hic salte![151]

---

[146] E. P. Thompson, 'Moral Economy Reviewed', in *Customs in Common* (London: Penguin Books, 1993), pp. 259–351 (pp. 339–40).

[147] D. W. Miller, *Queen's Rebels: Ulster Loyalism in Historical Perspective* (re-issued 1978 ed., Dublin: University College Dublin Press, 2007).

[148] Ibid., p. 119.

[149] A. J. Meyer, *The Persistence of the Old Regime: Europe to the Great War* (London: Croom Helm, 1981); R. Foster also utilises the term *ancien régime ancien* to describe Victorian Ireland in R. F. Foster, *W. B. Yeats: A Life*, 2 vols. (Oxford: Oxford University Press, 1997), I: *The Apprentice Mage, 1865–1914*, p. xxviii.

[150] See C. J. V. Loughlin, 'Representing Labour'.

[151] From *Aesop's Fables*, trans: 'Here is Rhodes, jump here!'

CHAPTER 2

Belfast Labour, Nationalism and Sectarianism

Abstract This chapter combines quantitative and qualitative analysis to examine the Belfast labour movement and national and religious division. It questions previous analysis—which has over-emphasised the 'failure' of labour in policy and electoral terms—on the politics of identity, nationality and sectarianism in the city. The first section is concerned with discussion of the politics of identity, nationality and sectarianism. It assesses the inter-war Belfast labour movement and the politics of nationality. The second section examines the relationship between the Belfast labour movement and sectarianism. It examines how national, political and sectarian violence and conflict affected local labour. The third section addresses how Belfast labour addressed sectarian rhetoric and language.

Keywords Belfast • Sectarianism • Political conflict and violence

> *In fact, the possibility of sectarian strife among workers was the nightmare of trade union organisers and they encountered it in a bewildering number of forms.*
> David Bleakley, 1980.[1]

---

[1] David Bleakley, *Saidie Patterson: Irish Peacemaker* (Belfast: Blackstaff Press, 1980), p. 29.

© The Author(s) 2018
C. J. V. Loughlin, *Labour and the Politics of Disloyalty in Belfast, 1921–39*, https://doi.org/10.1007/978-3-319-71081-5_2

The inter-war Belfast labour movement was forced to deal with two contentious aspects of the Northern Ireland question: the politics of sectarianism and nationality.[2] William McMullen, Northern Ireland Labour Party (NILP) MP, writing in 1926, stated 'we require to be frank enough to admit as a movement we have never had the courage to face the national question squarely'.[3] By the end of the 1930s, little more, it appeared, had been done to address the issue. J. R. Campbell, writing to the Belfast branch of the Communist Party of Ireland (CPI), despaired that 'in spite of the fighting traditions of the Belfast working class the labour movement has failed to take root there because it has pretended that this [national] question was not of decisive importance'.[4] Both William McMullen and J. R. Campbell identified the lack of a clear policy on the national question as the key reason for the meagre development of the Belfast labour movement. Such neglect was probably a response to the divisive nature of this question. The politics of nationality caused the severe polarisation of British and Irish politics in 1880–1920: Labour politics was similarly divided by such issues during the inter-war period.[5] We should therefore harbour less judgement about the failure of Belfast Labour during the inter-war period; Belfast and Northern Ireland still struggle with resolution of the contentious politics of identity.

Sectarianism in Northern Ireland—Christian-based, ethno-national conflict—has often been utilised as the master narrative to explain and account for the peculiar history of the region.[6] Within the academic literature, it is predominantly accepted that alongside the political division between Unionism and Nationalism, there was a division within the labour market in the north between predominantly skilled, Protestant workers

[2] Throughout this chapter, 'nationality', 'nationalism' and 'national question' will be used interchangeably.

[3] *The Voice of Labour*, 6 Feb. 1926; for autobiographical information on McMullen, see Gerry McElroy, 'William McMullen', in *Dictionary of Irish Biography* ed. by James McGuire and James Quinn (Cambridge: Cambridge University Press, 2009) <http://dib.cambridge.org> [accessed 1 May 2017].

[4] J. R. Campbell to members of the Belfast branch, Communist Party of Ireland, 18 Oct. 1938 (Dublin, Dublin City Archive, Communist Party of Ireland Papers, Box 4/016).

[5] Graham Walker, *The Politics of Frustration: Harry Midgley and the Failure of Labour in Northern Ireland* (Manchester: Manchester University Press, 1985), p. 15.

[6] See footnote 12, Chap. 4.

and largely unskilled, Catholic workers.[7] Division was further demonstrated by denominational influence within education and welfare services.[8]
The rhetoric and practice of the Northern Ireland state administration by
the Ulster Unionist Party (UUP) also gave a sectarian hue to the government. As C. G. Brown has commented, 'from the outset [Northern
Ireland] was Protestant dominated in numerical, political and institutional
terms'.[9] Angela Clifford further claimed that these divisions amounted to
two distinct civil societies in Northern Ireland.[10] Buckland has concurred
with such a view, stating that Catholics and Protestants lived apart in
mutual isolation.[11] The evidence presented below investigates the extent
to which an essentialised religious division was explicit in Belfast during
the inter-war period and it examines the intersection of the politics of
nationality, community and religion.

The Belfast labour movement created alternative structures to those
provided by other groups and the state. This involved the provision of
political, economic, social and educational organisations for working-class
people. The basis of the labour movement was thus one of a 'horizontal'
linkage of working-class people across one country and ultimately internationally.[12] This contrasts to the 'vertical' national division which united
members of different social classes and other groups within the nation.
This tension between a 'vertical' (national) division versus a 'horizontal'
(class) division lies at the heart of sectarianism in Belfast. Sectarianism was

[7] See, for example, Andrew Boyd, *Have the Trade-Unions Failed the North?* (Cork, 1984),
p. 61; Graham Walker, *The Politics of Frustration*, p. 15.

[8] Patrick Buckland, 'A Protestant State: Unionists in Government, 1921–39', in *Defenders
of the Union: A Survey of British and Irish Unionism since 1801* ed. by D. G. Boyce and Alan
O'Day (London: Routledge, 2001), p. 217; Erhard Rumpf and A. C. Hepburn, *Nationalism
and Socialism in Twentieth-Century Ireland* (Liverpool: Liverpool University Press, 1977),
p. 173.

[9] C. G. Brown, *Religion and Society in Twentieth Century Britain* (London: Pearson
Longman, 2006), p. 136.

[10] Angela Clifford, *Poor Law in Ireland: With an Account of the Belfast Outdoor Relief
Dispute, 1932 and the Development of the British Welfare State and Social Welfare in the
Republic* (Belfast: Athol Books, 1983), p. 21.

[11] Patrick Buckland, 'A Protestant State: Unionists in Government, 1921–39', in *Defenders
of the Union: A Survey of British and Irish Unionism since 1801* ed. by D. G. Boyce and Alan
O'Day (London: Routledge, 2001), pp. 211–26 (p. 217).

[12] Stefan Berger and Angel Smith, 'Between Scylla and Charybdis: Nationalism, Labour
and Ethnicity across Five Continents', in *Nationalism, Labour and Ethnicity, 1870–1939* ed.
by Stefan Berger and Angel Smith (Manchester: Manchester University Press, 1999),
pp. 1–30 (p. 6).

an expression of the 'vertical' division which was intimately related to issues of nationality, ethnicity and religion. These issues combined to prevent the development of a strong political Labour voice in the region.

The chapter below is divided into three sections. The first section is concerned with discussion of the politics of identity and nationality in inter-war Belfast. It assesses the Belfast labour movement and the politics of nationality. The second section will examine the relationship between the Belfast labour movement and sectarianism. How did the labour movement respond to sectarian conflict and violence? How was sectarian rhetoric used against the labour movement? The third section addresses: to what extent was anti-sectarian rhetoric used by the labour movement? Did the labour movement attempt to transcend sectarian division?

2.1   Section I: The Politics of Nationality and Sectarianism

The dilemma of nationality is political. Jonathan Tonge has interpreted the conflict in Ireland as a political problem of competing national identities where the division between these two identities 'is deepened by the religious, cultural and social divide which often coincides with the political divide'.[13] This concurs with Simon Prince and Geoffrey Warner's contention that 'the Troubles' from the 1960s onwards were primarily a political problem traceable to the incomplete nature of the Irish revolutionary process of the first quarter of the twentieth century.[14] Prior to the First World War, the politics of nationality became entwined with the question of Home Rule for Ireland.[15] The partition of Ireland, which resulted in new parliaments north and south of the border, and the Treaty of 1921, which resulted in the establishment of the Irish Free State, were the primary political events which shaped the context for inter-war Belfast labour politics. Inter-war Belfast labour had to deal with a number of issues linked to the national question: the relationship of Northern Ireland's labour organisation to that in the UK and Ireland; sectarianism; and partition.

---

[13] Jonathan Tonge, *Northern Ireland: Conflict and Change* (second ed., Harlow: Longman, 2002), p. 1.

[14] Simon Prince and Geoffrey Warner, *Belfast and Derry in Revolt: A New History of the Start of the Troubles* (Dublin: Irish Academic Press, 2012), p. 5.

[15] See section I of Chap. 1 above.

Here, the Belfast labour movement is defined as the political associations of labour and working-class organisations, communist organisations, the NILP, the Independent Labour Party (ILP), the Socialist Party of Northern Ireland (SPNI) and the Ulster Unionist Labour Association (UULA) and also the primary economic organisation of working-class people, the trade unions. The UULA is included as a subset of working-class political culture: a form of working-class conservatism.[16]

The definition used to examine sectarianism is Christian-based, ethno-religious conflict and violence. Sectarian politics and culture are complex because of the relationship these have to each other and wider issues of identity. Both Ulster Unionism and Irish Nationalism incorporated significant sectarian dimensions because of their social bases in opposing sides of the community divide. Religious, political and ethnic identities were each utilised as 'boundary markers' between Unionism and Nationalism in Northern Ireland.[17] They were, however, further used to delegitimise expression of autonomous labour identity. So, for example, the Ulster Unionists often pointed to the political association of Labour and Nationalism to prove the suspect nature of the former: a Shankill ward UUP advert in 1920 stated 'No Home Rule; No Socialism!'[18] An advert in the pro-Irish nationalist *Irish News* in 1933 appealed to Catholics to vote for neither the NILP nor UUP candidates as both had refused to condemn the partition of Ireland.[19]

Tim Wilson has recently claimed that acts of political violence in 1920–22 in Northern Ireland 'tended to be interpreted in terms of the overarching communal conflict'.[20] Therefore, according to Wilson, 'the prism of interpretation [of violence] was communal … to know the communal identity of the victim was to know the communal identity of the perpetrator'.[21] A communal interpretation was also applied to politics

[16] Graham Walker, 'The Northern Ireland Labour Party, 1924–45', in *Politics and the Irish Working Class, 1830–1945* ed. by Donal Ó Drisceoil and Fintan Lane (Basingstoke: Palgrave Macmillan, 2005), pp. 229–45 (p. 243).

[17] G. I. Higgins and J. D. Brewer, 'The Roots of Sectarianism in Northern Ireland', in *Researching the Troubles: Social Science Perspectives on the Northern Ireland Conflict* ed. by David Dickson and Owen Hargie (Edinburgh: Mainstream, 2003), pp. 107–21 (p. 108).

[18] *Belfast Newsletter*, 10 Jan. 1920.

[19] *Irish News*, 1 Dec. 1933.

[20] Timothy Wilson, *Frontiers of Violence: Conflict and Identity in Ulster and Upper Silesia 1918–22* (Oxford: Oxford University Press, 2010), p. 192.

[21] Ibid., p. 193.

more generally during the inter-war period in Belfast. Any co-operation by the labour movement with Unionism or Nationalism was interpreted as communal identification with these political blocs. As a result, the room for manoeuvre of the Belfast labour movement was highly circumscribed. An interesting example of how communal politics affected the Belfast labour movement is provided by Betty Sinclair's explanation for why Harry Midgley, NILP MP, lost his Dock ward seat in 1938. She claimed that 'people said he [Midgley] lost his Dock seat because he helped the Catholics ... he lost his seat because he deserted the Catholics [during the sectarian riots in 1935]'.[22] In a 'zero-sum'[23] conception of Northern Irish politics, either political position attributed to Harry Midgley—whether true or not—led to the alienation of, at least, one side of the communal divide.

2.1.1 Marx, Connolly and Walker

In the late nineteenth century, socialist and Marxist movements debated the politics of national self-determination. Marx and Engels had supported the demand for the independent statehood of Poland and Ireland, for example.[24] The Second International, in the early 1900s, further debated the politics of imperialism, colonialism and nationalism.[25] At the 1907 Stuttgart congress, the right wing of the International argued that colonies were justified by the progressive developments they made possible in backward countries.[26] But support for the dominant nationality against the subordinate nation was not confined to the right wing of the Second International. Rosa Luxemburg, associated with the left wing of the International, rejected independence for Poland from Russia as indicative of supporting one form of bourgeois rule against another.[27] Lenin, also associated with the left wing of the International, saw national

[22] Ronnie Munck and Bill Rolston, *Belfast in the Thirties: An Oral History* (Belfast: Blackstaff Press, 1987), p. 153.

[23] Timothy Wilson, *Frontiers of Violence*, p. 201.

[24] Anthony Coughlan, 'Ireland's Marxist Historians', in *Interpreting Irish History: The Debate on Historical Revisionism, 1938–1994* ed. by Ciaran Brady (Dublin: Irish Academic Press, 1994), pp. 288–305 (p. 292).

[25] The Second International was an international grouping of left-wing parties whose most significant period politically was 1889 to 1914. See Leszek Kolakowski, *Main Currents of Marxism: Its Rise, Growth and Dissolution*, 3 vols. (Oxford: Clarendon Press, 1978), II: *The Golden Age.*

[26] Kieran Allen, *The Politics of James Connolly* (London: Pluto Press, 1990), pp. 31–2.

[27] Leszek Kolakowski, *Main Currents of Marxism*, II: *The Golden Age*, pp. 90–2.

self-determination as progressive if it furthered development towards socialist revolution but reactionary if it stunted the development of socialist revolution. Another position on the national question was that adopted by Otto Bauer and Austrian Social-Democracy. They advocated 'cultural autonomy' within the confines of the multi-national Austro-Hungarian Empire. The significant point is that Marxism and the Second International did not have an agreed policy or politics on national self-determination. Similarly, neither advocacy of separation nor opposition to separation nor 'cultural autonomy' was explicitly associated with either the right or left of the Second International.

The contested politics of imperialism, colonialism, and national self-determination and the development of Irish Nationalism in the nineteenth century form the background to the James Connolly–William Walker controversy. The controversy was conducted through the pages of the Scottish ILP newspaper *Forward* between May and July 1911.[28] William Walker was the most significant labour politician produced by Belfast in the 20 years prior to the First World War[29], whilst James Connolly was the most important Irish Marxist of the twentieth century and worked as an organiser for the Irish Transport and General Workers' Union (ITGWU) in Belfast in 1910–14.[30] What were the issues at stake in the debate?

The Connolly-Walker debate centred on the question of independent labour organisation in Ireland.[31] In anticipation of Home Rule, which Connolly viewed as furthering the development of class antagonisms within Ireland and thus to be supported from a Marxist perspective, those influenced by Connolly advocated the setting up of an Irish Labour Party independent of British labour structures. Walker accepted the need for independent labour representation, but he argued that this representation should take place within the more developed British labour movement.

[28] Austen Morgan, *Labour and Partition: The Belfast Working Class, 1905–23* (London: Pluto Press, 1991), pp. 147–9.

[29] For autobiographical information on William Walker, see L. W. White, 'William Walker', in *Dictionary of Irish Biography* ed. by James McGuire and James Quinn (Cambridge: Cambridge University Press, 2009) <http://dib.cambridge.org> [accessed 1 May 2017].

[30] There are a myriad of publications dealing with Connolly; some of the more important are C. D. Greaves, *The Life and Times of James Connolly* (London: Lawrence and Wishart, 1961); Austen Morgan, *James Connolly: A Political Biography* (Manchester: Manchester University Press, 1988); Donal Nevin, *James Connolly: A Full Life* (Dublin: Gill & Macmillan, 2005); see also footnote 33 below.

[31] See Cork Workers Club, *The Connolly-Walker Controversy on Socialist Unity in Ireland* (Cork: Cork Workers Club, 1974).

Connolly, however, saw Walker as subjugating the political development of Ireland to Britain. William Walker, in Connolly's assessment, was acting as an apologist for an imperialist viewpoint and was therefore a Labour Imperialist. In 1912, four of the five Belfast ILP branches split from the British ILP to help form the ILP (Ireland) in conjunction with James Connolly.[32] Following his execution by the British military for his role in the 1916 Easter Rising, James Connolly entered the pantheon of Irish separatist martyrs.[33]

The Connolly-Walker debate presaged the organisational divisions which occurred in the Irish labour movement in 1909–23. The Belfast Trades Council, for example, disaffiliated from the Irish Trades Union Congress in 1912 in response to the latter's decision to set up an Irish Labour Party. When the Irish National Teachers' Organisation in 1918 aligned itself with the national independence movement, teachers in the north split and founded the Ulster Teachers' Union (UTU). Similarly, many southern Irish trade unions split from their sister British organisations in 1917–23. The significant ITGWU expansion in this period was geographically concentrated in counties which would form the Irish Free State; it never gained a large number of members in the six counties that formed Northern Ireland in 1921.[34]

Connolly and Walker bequeathed an ambiguous legacy to the Belfast labour movement: independent working-class labour politics but contrasting interpretations of the politics of nationality. Some analysts have claimed that the NILP and trade unions were vague on the national question in Ireland.[35] Rather, there was no definitive position on the national question. As a result, individuals and political groupings within the Belfast labour movement each had their own respective position on the politics of nationalism. It is significant, in this context, that no important theoretical work on the national question was produced by left-wing activists in

---

[32] Austen Morgan, *Labour & Partition*, p. 149.

[33] The exact balance between socialism and republicanism within James Connolly's life and thought is a contentious and massive topic. For the definitive introduction to the key literature, see Conor McCabe and Emmet O'Connor, 'Ireland', in *Histories of Labour: National and International Perspectives* ed. by Joan Allen, Alan Campbell, and John McIlroy (Pontypool: The Merlin Press, 2010), pp. 137–63; and footnote 30 above.

[34] Emmet O'Connor, *A Labour History of Ireland, 1824–2000* (second revised ed., Dublin: University College Dublin Press, 2011), pp. 108–9.

[35] Ronnie Munck and Bill Rolston, *Belfast in the Thirties*, pp. 131–2; Erhard Rumpf and A. C. Hepburn, *Nationalism & Socialism*, p. 241.

Belfast over the course of the inter-war period. The Belfast labour movement had no agreed position on the national question and this is because groupings within it were themselves divided by the national question. We should note, however, that Marxism remained underdeveloped theoretically on nationalism until, at least, the 1960s. Therefore, Belfast labour's failure on the above issue may be indicative of a wider underdevelopment of working-class political thought.

2.1.1.1 Belfast Labour and the Politics of Nationality, 1921–39

How was the politics of nationality manifested in the inter-war Belfast labour movement? The violent partition of Ireland witnessed workplace expulsions in east Ulster and this posed difficulties for Labour in Ireland. The violence, in 1920–22, severely hampered the Belfast labour movement and this, combined with the abolition of Single Transferable Vote proportional representation for local government elections, witnessed the decline of Labour-associated councillors in Belfast from 12 in 1920 to just two by 1924.[36] Inter-war trade unions were also divided by where they were headquartered: in Britain, Belfast or Dublin. Splits had occurred prior to partition, as detailed above, but contention remained. The difficulties involved in resolving these issues were even replicated amongst communists. The official position adopted by the Profintern, the communist trade union international, was that the English trade unions should withdraw from Ireland.[37] Harry Pollitt, of the Communist Party of Great Britain, disagreed. He argued in 1925 that it was tactically wrong as it would be used 'as a weapon' by 'reactionary trade union leaders' to undermine the work of comrades in the Minority Movement[38] in Britain.[39] This position hardened after Jim Larkin attacked the policy of the British Minority Movement at their conference in August 1925. Pollitt responded that no one saw the proposal for British trade union withdrawal from Ireland as practical and that 'the thousands of workers who are bound up

---

[36] See Chap. 3 below.

[37] Harry Pollitt to A. Losovosky, 12 Jan. 1925 (Queen's University Belfast, Northern Ireland, Comintern papers, MS57/6/4/534/6/79/20-2) (copies of Comintern files from 495, ECCI, held in the Russian State Archive for Social and Political History (Rossiiskii Gosudartsvennyi Arkhiv Sotsial'no-Politischesko Istorii fondi)).

[38] The Minority Movement was a communist-inspired attempt to organise a radical, left-wing presence within trade unions in Britain.

[39] Harry Pollitt to A. Losovosky, 5 Feb. 1925 (QUB, Comintern papers, MS57/6/5/534/26/39).

with British trade unions [in Ireland] ... would never dream of voluntarily withdrawing from these unions'.[40] At the 1930 NILP annual conference, the Belfast Court ward Labour Party tabled a resolution, which was defeated, calling for the expulsion of British-based trade unions from Ireland.[41] Similarly, there was bitter conflict in the 1930s between the ITGWU and the British-based Amalgamated Transport & General Workers' Union.[42] The position of British-based unions in southern Ireland in the 1930s became more difficult when a Trade Union Commission of Inquiry called for the expulsion of these unions from Ireland.[43]

During the inter-war period, members of the NILP were free to advocate their own view on the politics of nationality. It was only in 1949 that the party definitively accepted the partition of Ireland. This compromise proved useful during the inter-war period as political positions on the border had yet to settle into rigid dogmatism. For example, a later British labourist, Harry Midgley, was anti-partitionist during the Northern Ireland general election of 1921 and Westminster elections of 1923 and 1924. Despite Midgley's anti-partitionism in the 1920s, he became more associated with British labour politics during the course of the inter-war period. Subsequently, he split from the NILP in 1942 and set up the pro–British Empire Commonwealth Labour Party; ultimately, Midgley joined the UUP and ended his political career as minister for education in Sir Basil Brooke's Northern Ireland cabinet.[44] William McMullen, a contemporary of James Connolly, consciously advocated an anti-partitionist Connollyite approach throughout his political career and in the trade union movement. McMullen was also involved with the Republican Congress. In the mid to late 1930s, the SPNI included members (such as Victor Halley) who advocated a Connollyite approach.[45] In 1938, Jack MacGougan, SPNI member, contested the Oldpark ward for the NILP whilst deploying distinctly anti-partitionist and republican rhetoric.[46]

[40] Harry Pollitt to A. Losovosky, 2 Sept. 1925 (QUB, Comintern papers, MS57/6/5/534/7/26/156).

[41] *The Irishman*, 26 April 1930.

[42] Boyd Black, 'British Trade Unions in Ireland', *Industrial Relations Journal*, 20, No. 2 (Summer 1989), 140–9 (141).

[43] Ibid.

[44] Graham Walker, *The Politics of Frustration*.

[45] Set up on 1 Jan. 1933 as a successor to the Northern Irish Independent Labour Party because of its parent bodies' disaffiliation from the British Labour Party the previous year.

[46] See electoral politics chapter below, p. 133.

What should be noted is the fluidity of these political positions. It should also be noted that compromise on the national question was experienced by republican-oriented activists as a positive reason for involvement with the NILP. In the 1980s, Jack MacGougan reminisced that 'we were able to … abide it [the NILP] as long as there was freedom of conscience on the constitutional question'.[47]

The contested legacies of James Connolly and William Walker were expressed in the inter-war Belfast labour movement. Graham Walker has argued that, ideologically speaking, Connolly's influence was 'far greater than that of [William] Walker'.[48] However, British labourist politics and organisation demonstrably influenced the Belfast labour movement: for example, the NILP founding constitution[49] replicated the British Labour Party's Clause IV.[50] The tendency of the NILP to identify with the British labour movement was also expressed through the prominence of trade union officials of British-based unions, such as Sam Kyle, and the importance given to public meetings at which British Labour Party MPs, such as David Kirkwood, spoke.[51] Kyle expressed this commitment to the Union when he advocated that the conditions of teachers, pensioners and the unemployed should not be lowered to the level then prevalent in the Irish Free State.[52] The NILP was initially given a lukewarm response by the Irish Labour Party because the latter organisation considered itself the legitimate political party for the whole island, north and south of the border.[53] The summer of 1926 witnessed an agreement between the northern and southern Irish Labour Parties to co-operate in an all-Ireland organisation.[54] This relationship, however, failed to become institutionally

---

[47] Ronnie Munck and Bill Rolston, *Belfast in the Thirties*, p. 149.

[48] Graham Walker, *The Politics of Frustration*, p. 49.

[49] *The Voice of Labour*, 21 Aug. 1926.

[50] Clause IV, the 'socialist' clause, was adopted by the British Labour Party in 1918. See *The Voice of Labour*, 21 Aug. 1926. The founding constitution of the NILP can be examined in C. J. V. Loughlin, 'The Political Culture of the Belfast Labour Movement, 1924–39', Queen's University Belfast PhD thesis, 2013, Appendix A, pp. 367–75.

[51] *The Labour Opposition of Northern Ireland*, Nov. 1925; for consideration of the relationship between labour in Ulster and Scotland, see Graham Walker, *Intimate Strangers: Political and Cultural Interaction Between Scotland and Ulster in Modern Times* (Edinburgh: John Donald, 1995).

[52] *The Labour Opposition of Northern Ireland*, April 1925.

[53] Irish Labour Party and Trades' Union Congress, *30th Annual Report* (Dublin: National Executive ILP & TUC, 1925), p. 164.

[54] *The Voice of Labour*, 17, 24 and 31 July 1926.

embedded; only twice did the Irish Free State Labour Party pay the promised subvention to the NILP.[55] In 1930, a new understanding was reached which essentially put the northern and southern Labour Parties into a fraternal relationship much like that which existed between the British Labour Party and the two Irish Labour Parties. *The Irishman*, the ITGWU's newspaper, commented bitterly that:

> To adopt, even in complete good faith, language and tactics originating in another country, whether it be a close neighbour or be far removed, is not to help forward the cause of labour in Ireland or of Irish unity.[56]

Tension over the NILP's policy on the national question continued in the 1930s. During the decade, the party developed closer links with the British Labour party.[57] This may have been reinforced by the southern Irish Labour Party's support for Fianna Fáil governments. Divisions over the national question were expressed most acutely at the 1937 NILP annual conference.[58] The Armagh branch sought to align the NILP more closely to the southern Labour Party, while the Belfast City Labour Party branch sought to keep the NILP in co-operation with 'the labour movements throughout the British Commonwealth of Nations'.[59] The NILP voted for the Belfast City Labour Party's resolution. This stance was reinforced at the 1938 NILP special conference when a new constitution was adopted. This gave the party a greater British bias.[60] Critics of the policy argued that this would alienate the Nationalist community from the NILP,[61] a view which seems to have been vindicated by the successes registered by left-wing, Irish-associated formations in Belfast after the Second World War.

The UULA maintained a distinct defence of the link with Britain. J. F. Gordon[62] stated that the UULA's principal aim was to maintain the

[55] Aaron Edwards, *A History of the Northern Ireland Labour Party: Democratic Socialism and Sectarianism* (Manchester: Manchester University Press, 2009), p. 16.

[56] *The Irishman*, 26 April 1930.

[57] Graham Walker, *The Politics of Frustration*, p. 60.

[58] Ibid., pp. 100–1.

[59] *Irish Democrat*, 6 Nov. 1937.

[60] *Workers' Republic*, June 1938.

[61] Ibid.

[62] J. F. Gordon, originally from Ireland, was educated in the USA and became a flax manager in Kildare and Meath. He represented the UUP on Belfast Corporation, 1920–23, and was elected a Northern Ireland House of Commons MP in 1921. He was parliamentary

legislative union with Britain.[63] While not solely a working-class organisation (the organisation's chairman for many years was J. M. Andrews, a
wealthy linen manufacturer and Northern Ireland cabinet member), it did
represent a genuine strand of working-class opinion. Graham Walker has
contended that Unionist labourism was the Northern Ireland form of
British working-class, social Toryism.[64] Austen Morgan has concurred,
'Labour Unionism was working class conservatism'.[65] Doubt has been cast
on the 30,000 membership claimed by the UULA across Northern
Ireland,[66] but the organisation did have a mass membership and influence
over a substantial section of the working class. The UULA also adopted
explicit sectarian positions. For example, in August 1921, a resolution was
passed unanimously by the UULA Executive which stated that the organisation 'viewed with alarm the filteration of Papists into Executive positions under the departments of our Northern parliament and call upon
our Prime Minister—Sir James Craig—and the cabinet to see that none
but Loyalists are elected to these positions and Protestants in preference'.[67]
Nationalism had no equivalent organisation, although the appeal of Joe
Devlin and the Ancient Order of Hibernians in Belfast was based, at least
partly, on a similar populist appeal to working-class Nationalists.[68]

The policies adopted by communists in Ireland meant that it was relatively easy for Unionist opponents to portray them as identified with Irish
Nationalism. The Marxist advocacy of independence for Ireland led communists on the island to advocate an all-Ireland Workers' Republic during

secretary to the Minister of Labour during the inter-war period and served as the Minister of
Labour from 1938 to 1943. See J. F. Harbinson, 'The Ulster Unionist Party, 1882–1970'
(unpublished PhD thesis, Queen's University Belfast, 1972), p. 295.

[63] J. F. Gordon to Viscount Craigavon, 14 April 1928 (Public Records Office of Northern
Ireland, Belfast, Northern Ireland (PRONI), Department of Prime Minister files, PM/6/32).

[64] Graham Walker, 'The Northern Ireland Labour Party, 1924–45', p. 243.

[65] Austen Morgan, *Labour & Partition*, p. 320.

[66] J. D. Clarkson, *Labour and Nationalism in Ireland* (New York: Columbia University
Press, 1925), p. 374.

[67] Ulster Unionist Labour Association Minutes, 6 Aug. 1921 (PRONI, Ulster Unionist
Council papers, D/1327/11/4/1).

[68] Enda Staunton, *The Nationalists of Northern Ireland* (Dublin: Columba Press, 2001),
pp. 9–10 and p. 113. A more favourable assessment of Devlin's appeal is contained in A. C.
Hepburn, *Catholic Belfast and Nationalist Ireland in the Era of Joe Devlin, 1871–1934*
(Oxford: Oxford University Press, 2008), pp. 4–6 (pp. 281–2); and Eamonn Phoenix,
*Northern Nationalism: Nationalist Politics, Partition and the Catholic Minority in Northern
Ireland, 1890–1940* (Belfast: Ulster Historical Foundation, 1994), pp. 2–6.

the inter-war period.[69] The policy of communists in Belfast was an application of Comintern policy but also at times reflected the changing conditions within Ireland. Under the impact of 'third period' communism in 1932, communists in Belfast advocated an all-Ireland anti-imperialist struggle north and south for an independent Workers' Republic. Comintern policy was revised during the mid-1930s to deal with the threat of fascism. At the Republican Congress in September 1934, communists advocated a united front for an independent united Ireland.[70] The People's Front policy adopted at the seventh world congress of the Comintern in August 1935 was also applied in Ireland. The creation of the Progressive Unionist Party by W. J. Stewart in 1937 appeared to herald an opportunity for a 'progressive' government at Stormont. In June 1937, William McCullough, a leading member of the Belfast CPI, called for the replacement of 'the official Unionist gang with a progressive government at Stormont'.[71] While the CPI was influenced by broader international communist strategy, it was granted significant flexibility in how to apply these political positions to the Irish context.[72]

In conclusion, the Belfast labour movement during the inter-war period had no definitive position on the national question. This was a result of labour being a movement rather than a single political party. As can be seen above, all of the political groupings in the Belfast labour movement

[69] The first two Irish affiliates to the Comintern from Ireland—the Roddy Connolly–led CPI (founded in 1921, following the renaming of the Socialist Party of Ireland) and the Jim Larkin–led Workers' Party of Ireland in the mid-1920s—had little to no presence in Northern Ireland. In the mid-1920s in Belfast, individuals such as Murtagh Morgan and Tommie Geehan were involved in a local branch of the communist-affiliated International Class War Prisoners' Aid. The third Comintern Irish affiliate, the 1933 CPI, did have a significant group based in Belfast. See Emmet O'Connor, *Reds and the Green: Ireland, Russia and the Communist Internationals, 1919–43* (Dublin: University College Dublin Press, 2004), pp. 51, 121 (pp. 179–94).

[70] Richard English, *Radicals and the Republic: Socialist Republicanism in the Irish Free State, 1925–37* (Oxford: Oxford University Press, 1994), p. 218.

[71] William McCullough, quoted in Mike Milotte, *Communism in Modern Ireland*, p. 179.

[72] This interpretation is broadly the thesis of Emmet O'Connor, *Reds and the Green*. See also the recent research on the Comintern and Britain in Alan Campbell and John McIlroy, 'Britain: The Twentieth-Century', in *Histories of Labour: National and International Perspectives* ed. by Joan Allen, Alan Campbell, and John McIlroy (Pontypool: The Merlin Press, 2010), p. 113. See also Seán Byers, 'Seán Murray's Political Apprenticeship: The Making of an Irish Republican Bolshevik', Saothar, 37 (2012), pp. 41–55; Seán Byers, *Seán Murray: Marxist-Leninist and Irish Socialist Republican* (Dublin: Irish Academic Press, 2015).

had their own position on the national question. The NILP decision to allow freedom of conscience on the issue was a useful compromise during the inter-war period. The lack of position adopted by the NILP, when compared with communists or the UULA, seems better suited to the politics of divided nationality. However, fraternal relations between different sections of the labour movement proved difficult to develop seriously during the inter-war period.

2.2   SECTION II: BELFAST LABOUR AND THE POLITICS OF SECTARIANISM

How did the Belfast labour movement respond to sectarian conflict and violence? 'Conflict' refers to protest through politics, assemblies, strikes and non-violent action, whereas 'violence' refers to riots, pogroms and civil wars.[73] The next section is broken into three chronological periods: Belfast labour responses prior to significant sectarian violence before and during the foundation of Northern Ireland (up to 1923); the response during the relatively quiescent period when only sectarian conflict took place (1924–33); and the labour response (1934–39) when significant sectarian violence again occurred in Belfast.

The ethos of the labour movement predisposed it to anti-sectarianism: the expulsion of Catholic or Protestant workers from their employment was inherently dangerous for the movement. Labour organisations were built on an acceptance of the solidarity of workers across workplaces. Speaking in 1893, for example, Sam Munro stated that 'trade unionism is the ism ... whose mission it shall be to free our unhappy land from the incubus of religious bigotry and religious intolerance'.[74] The founding manifesto of the ILP (Ireland) stated that the issue was not one of religion or ethnicity but '*all workers against all exploiters*'.[75] Sectional, craft and gender divisions did compete with class, but the assumption of 'new unionists' and syndicalist labour activists, such as Larkin and Connolly, was working-class consciousness and the syndicalist conception of 'one big

---

[73] Ashutosh Varshney, 'Ethnicity and Ethnic Conflict', in *The Oxford Handbook of Comparative Politics* ed. by Carles Boix and S. C. Stokes (Oxford: Oxford University Press, 2007), p. 279.

[74] Quoted in Terry Cradden, 'The Trade Union Movement in Northern Ireland', in *Trade Union Century* ed. by Donal Nevin (Cork: Mercier Press, 1994), p. 69.

[75] Quoted in Kieran Allen, *Connolly*, p. 107.

union'. This posed a number of difficult issues for older, more well-established trade unions.

Between 1850 and 1924, sectarian conflict and violence broke out in Belfast on six occasions: 1857, 1864, 1886, 1893, 1912 and 1920.[76] Sectarian division was undoubtedly a significant driver of violence, but to account for why and who was expelled from work and home requires a political explanation. Significantly, in 1912 and 1920, *both* Catholics and Protestants who dissented from Loyalism were expelled from workplaces.[77] Austen Morgan has estimated that in 1912 Protestants constituted 20% of the 2000–3000 expelled from work and in 1920 25% of the 7000–8000 ejected from their employment.[78] The expulsion of both Catholic and Protestant workers points towards the political nature of this violence. The expulsion of workers was a matter of severe contention and threatened to cripple cross-community politics. Labour's credibility as a political and economic alternative was also damaged because of the lack of a clear response. In 1912, Roman Catholic clergy and Joe Devlin, MP, organised a vigilance committee to resist expulsions.[79] James Connolly, however, argued that trade unions should oppose sectarianism on a non-communal basis. His union, the ITGWU, attempted this but no other unions responded to Connolly's initiative.[80] This exemplifies the Belfast labour movement's response to sectarian conflict and violence: the issue was so contentious that a centralised and co-ordinated response was close to impossible. For example, at the end of July 1920, only two members out of the 12-member labour group on Belfast Corporation turned up at the specially convened corporation meeting to protest at workplace expulsions.[81] In September 1920, the Amalgamated Society of Woodworkers (ASW) struck for the re-instatement of expelled members. However, only

---

[76] See Catherine Hirst, *Religion, Politics and Violence in Nineteenth-Century Belfast: The Pound and Sandy Row* (Dublin: Four Courts, 2001); Mark Doyle, *Fighting like the Devil for the Sake of God: Protestants, Catholics and the Origins of Violence in Victorian Belfast* (Manchester: Manchester University Press, 2009).

[77] Boyd Black, 'Reassessing Irish Industrial Relations and Labour History: The North-East of Ireland up to 1921', *Historical Studies in Industrial Relations*, 14 (Autumn 2002), 45–97 (60); Erhard Rumpf and A. C. Hepburn, *Nationalism & Socialism*, p. 198.

[78] Austen Morgan, 'Politics, the Labour Movement and the Working Class in Belfast, 1905–23' (unpublished PhD thesis, Queen's University Belfast, 1978), pp. 124 and 212.

[79] Kieran Allen, *James Connolly*, p. 110.

[80] Ibid.

[81] Emmet O'Connor, *A Labour History of Ireland, 1824–2000*, pp. 191–2.

500–600 ASW members struck and as a result the union executive expelled the majority of its own membership for strike breaking.[82] In 1929, the Belfast Trades Council claimed that:

> In Ireland [1920–2] there came what is now referred to as 'the trouble.' It was not Labour's fault, and it was not Labour's fight! Suffice it to say that the atmosphere was such that the Belfast Trades' [sic] Council had no option but to become quiescent during a very troublous period in Ireland's history.[83]

In short, a policy of inaction, which amounted to acquiescence, was adopted by the majority of trade unionists. A significant and radical minority, however, such as James Connolly and Jim Larkin when based in Belfast, attempted to resist sectarian violence. The most detailed analysis of the 1920 workplace expulsions is the research conducted by Austen Morgan and Christopher Norton.[84] Norton emphasised, like Henry Patterson, the economic vulnerability of those responsible for the expulsions.[85] This is in contrast to authors, such as Michael Farrell and Geoffrey Bell, who explained the expulsions as a result of the privileged position of Protestant workers.[86] Supporting Norton's interpretation, labour activists later alleged that the UUP encouraged demobilised soldiers to 'clear the Catholics out' if they wanted a job.[87] Norton has also argued that Loyalism gained only a temporary ascendancy within the trade unions and was unable to extinguish the Labourist tradition of the Belfast working class.[88] Although the Expelled Workers'

[82] Austen Morgan, *Labour & Partition*, p. 282.
[83] Belfast Trades' and Labour Council, *Souvenir of the Trades Union Congress at the Grosvenor Hall Belfast, September 1929* (Belfast: Wm. Strain & Sons, 1929), p. 76.
[84] Austen Morgan, *Labour & Partition*, pp. 265–84; Christopher Norton, 'Unionist Politics, the Belfast Shipyards and the Labour Movement in the Inter-War Period' (unpublished D.Phil. thesis, University of Ulster, 1987); Christopher Norton, 'Worker Response to the 1920 Belfast Shipyard Expulsions', *Études-Irelandaises*, (Spring 1996), 153–63; A. F. Parkinson, *Belfast's Unholy War: The Troubles of the 1920s* (Dublin: Four Courts Press, 2004).
[85] Henry Patterson, 'Industrial Labour and the Labour Movement, 1820–1914', in *An Economic History of Ulster, 1820–1939* ed. by Liam Kennedy and Philip Ollerenshaw (Manchester: Manchester University Press, 1985), pp. 158–83 (p. 178).
[86] Geoffrey Bell, *The Protestants of Ulster* (London, 1976); Michael Farrell, *Northern Ireland: The Orange State* (revised second ed., London, 1980).
[87] *The Voice of Labour*, 8 Dec. 1923.
[88] Christopher Norton, 'The 1920 Belfast Shipyard Expulsions', p. 158.

Committee was led by two Labourists, James Baird[89] and John Hanna, most support given to the Committee came from 'Catholic, Nationalist and Sinn Féin sources'.[90] This may be considered natural given that the majority of those expelled were Catholic. The expulsions were also a blow to the collectivist ethos of 'new unionism' and syndicalism. The criterion for expulsion, however, was what was considered politically 'disloyal'. Boyd Black has concluded that 'the decisive criterion [for expulsion] was political rather than simply religious'.[91] What is significant is that this violence set a 'Protestant political economy' to the economics and politics of the Northern Ireland[92]; only Loyalists and Unionists could guarantee their safety within local society. The politics of Northern Ireland was founded upon majoritarian conceptions and a lack of regard for the rights of minorities: it was fundamentally a moral economy of loyalty.

2.2.1   The Response to Sectarian Conflict, 1924–33

Conflict between the Belfast labour movement and opposing political forces took place frequently, though not incessantly, throughout the interwar period. Templemore Avenue in east Belfast, for example, was a flashpoint in the 1930s between labour and loyalists. An Outdoor Relief Workers' meeting had to be called off in June 1931 because of intimidation by Loyalist drumming parties.[93] In September 1931, Captain Jack White,[94] along with three communists, was arrested while leading a communist procession into east Belfast. On 10 September 1931, the communists were prevented from holding a meeting at Templemore Avenue because of a Loyalist drumming party. On Friday 16 September 1931, a mass meeting of 2000 people at the Custom House steps resolved to march on the disputed locality the next day. The police claimed that a

---

[89] James Baird was a boilermaker by trade who emigrated from Ireland to Australia in 1924; he died there in 1948. See Emmet O'Connor, *A Labour History of Ireland, 1824–2000*, p. 191.

[90] Ibid., p. 192.

[91] Boyd Black, 'Reassessing Irish Industrial Relations', p. 60.

[92] Austen Morgan, *Labour & Partition*, p. 271.

[93] Inspector General's Office to Secretary, Ministry of Home Affairs, 30 June 1931(PRONI, Ministry of Home Affairs files, HA/32/1/546).

[94] Captain James Robert 'Jack' White was born in County Antrim and was a key figure in the pre-First World War Irish Citizen Army (ICA). See Fearghal McGarry, 'James Robert 'Jack' White' *Dictionary of Irish Biography* ed. by James McGuire and James Quinn (Cambridge: Cambridge University Press, 2009) <dib.cambridge.org> [accessed 1 May 2017].

crowd of 400, with 300 hangers-on, assembled to march on Templemore Avenue.[95] When the communist procession reached Queen's Bridge, red flags were furled at the request of the police.[96] At the corner of the Newtownards Road and Templemore Avenue, a drumming party accompanied by (depending on which source you believe) 400[97] or 2000[98] people met the communist procession. When Captain Jack White attempted to break through police lines, the police responded by baton-charging the communists. Captain White alleged that this 'was perfectly obvious shameless partisanship on the part of the force'.[99] At a protest meeting at Berlin Street a few days later, Loyalists affirmed their rejection of communism and devotion to King and Empire.[100] Templemore Avenue highlights the politics of territory in Belfast. However, one year later, the Templemore Avenue area of Belfast had representatives on the Outdoor Relief Workers' Committee and witnessed demonstrations in support of the demands of the unemployed.[101] The events of 1932 point to the malleability of politics in Belfast and Northern Ireland. Politics was continually contested, whether by independent Unionists, nationalists and republicans or from left-wing challenges. Loyalism and the UUP were dominant, but this did not amount to a hegemony. Politics in Belfast was a police action[102] and this further highlights the non-consensual nature of the political order created in the region.

2.2.2   Belfast Labour and Sectarian Violence, 1934–39

While some research has been carried out on the riots of May-August 1935, less attention has been paid to the events of the previous two years.

[95] Inspector General's Office to Secretary, Ministry of Home Affairs, 17 Sept. 1931(PRONI, Ministry of Home Affairs files, HA/32/1/546).

[96] *Belfast Telegraph*, 22 Sept. 1931; *Irish News*, 18 Sept. 1931.

[97] *Irish News*, 18 Sept. 1931.

[98] The figure is typed '200' with a further zero written in ink to give the figure of 2000. It is unclear whether this figure was mistyped or deliberately changed. See Inspector General's Office to Secretary, Ministry of Home Affairs, 17 Sept. 1931(PRONI, Ministry of Home Affairs files, HA/32/1/546).

[99] *Irish News*, 18 Sept. 1931.

[100] *Belfast Telegraph*, 22 Sept. 1931.

[101] Inspector General's Office to Secretary, Ministry of Home Affairs, 12 Sept., 6 and 10 Oct. 1932 (PRONI, Ministry of Home Affairs files, HA/8/276).

[102] Jacques Rancière, Disagreement: Politics and Philosophy (Minnesota: University of Minnesota Press, 2004), p. xiii.

This is despite discussion of the notorious sectarian statements by leading members of the UUP in the 1930s. In 1933, Sir Basil Brooke, the Northern Ireland Minister of Agriculture, declared that he would not employ Catholics but would rather have good Protestant 'lads and lassies'.[103] Brooke's statement was described, justifiably, by communists as a deliberate incitement to sectarianism.[104] The following year, Brooke explained why he would not employ Catholics: they were '99% disloyal'.[105] Similarly, Craigavon, who backed the statement of his cabinet colleague,[106] declared: 'All I boast of is that we are a Protestant parliament and a Protestant state'.[107] A meeting of the CPI at Berlin Street in April 1934 condemned 'Craigavon's new divide and conquer drive'.[108] The article called on all trade union and labour bodies to protest against sectarianism because 'the working class is the class for whom this provocation has the greatest danger'.[109] At the end of May 1934, Tommie Geehan, the foremost Belfast communist of the 1930s, drew attention to the role of the ultra-Loyalist Ulster Protestant League (UPL)[110] and its newspaper the *Ulster Protestant*:

> I was fairly convinced that the functions and the duty of this paper was to set about organising another religious pogrom in this city … all the paper contains is a vicious and scurrilous attack on the religion of the minority.[111]

The CPI in Belfast followed a deliberate policy of pointing out the dangers of sectarianism. However, only the CPI's newspaper, the *Irish Workers' Voice*, printed a letter signed by five trade unions, Harry Midgley and the Irish Unemployed Workers' Movement (IUWM) which condemned

---

[103] Quoted in Michael Farrell, *Northern Ireland*, p. 90.

[104] Inspector General's Office to Secretary, Ministry of Home Affairs, 11 April 1934 (PRONI, Ministry of Home Affairs files, HA/32/1/550).

[105] Basil Brooke, quoted in *Belfast Newsletter*, 20 March 1934; quoted at 'Discrimination—Quotations' <cain.ulst.ac.uk/issues/discrimination/quotes.htm> [accessed 1 March 2017]; also, see above, Chap. 1, footnote 56.

[106] Michael Farrell, *Northern Ireland*, p. 91.

[107] *Hansard N.I. (Commons)*, xvi, 1095 (24 April 1934).

[108] *Irish Workers' Voice*, 7 April 1934.

[109] Ibid., 31 March, 7 and 28 April, 2 June 1934.

[110] Graham Walker, '"Protestantism before Party!": The Ulster Protestant League in the 1930s', *The Historical Journal*, xxviii, No. 4 (1985), 961–7.

[111] Inspector General's Office to Secretary, Ministry of Home Affairs, 31 May 1934 (PRONI, Ministry of Home Affairs files, HA/32/1/550).

attempts to incite sectarian consciousness.[112] Sectarian tension in Belfast is further alluded to by the communist contention in September 1934 that a 'gang of hooligans' tried to intimidate workers out of the shipyard.[113] In response, representatives of the ASW met Sir Dawson Bates and threatened a general strike if adequate protection was not given to workers at the shipyard.[114] However, the *Irish Workers' Voice* claimed that pogrom efforts had failed in Belfast.[115] It is reasonable to conclude that the Belfast labour movement may well have prevented more significant sectarian conflict and violence from developing.

Yet sectarian violence gripped Belfast between May and August 1935. That year began with a significant dispute between Belfast labour and the authorities over the prosecution of Tommie Geehan for defying a ban on the commemoration of the Outdoor Relief riots of 1932. In February and March 1935, big demonstrations were held in aid of Geehan's case and also in opposition to the implementation of the 1934 Unemployment Act.[116] In May 1935, the silver jubilee of King George V occurred. Reproduced below are two photographs from the pro-UUP *Belfast Telegraph* of workplaces in Belfast during the jubilee. The pictures highlight the politicised nature of employment space in inter-war Northern Ireland. It demonstrates how one form of identity, the British, was legitimised in Northern Ireland while alternative expressions of political identity were therefore considered 'disloyal' (Figs. 2.1 and 2.2).

The tensions in Belfast in May 1935 are illustrated by the fact that IRA members and the secretary of the UPL were observed by the police attending the Communist Mayday rally.[117] Presumably, both organisations attended to gather information on the communists in Belfast. At a meeting on 5 May, UPL members heckled and interrupted the IUWM.[118] The UPL members who gathered on 12 May, the communists having decided

[112] Ibid., 9 June 1934.
[113] Inspector General's Office to Secretary, Ministry of Home Affairs, 28 Sept. 1934 (PRONI, Ministry of Home Affairs files, HA/32/1/550).
[114] Ibid.
[115] *Irish Workers' Voice*, 29 Sept. 1934.
[116] Inspector General's Office to Ministry of Home Affairs, 16 Oct. 1934 (PRONI, Ministry of Home Affairs files, HA/32/1/550); Inspector General's Office to Ministry of Home Affairs, 7 Nov. 1934 (PRONI, Ministry of Home Affairs files, HA/32/1/551).
[117] Inspector General's Office to Secretary, Ministry of Home Affairs, 2 May 1935 (PRONI, Ministry of Home Affairs files, HA/32/1/552).
[118] Inspector General's Office to Secretary, Ministry of Home Affairs, 7 May 1935 (PRONI, Ministry of Home Affairs files, HA/32/1/553).

Fig. 2.1   Belfast Collar Company premises, May 1935 (*Belfast Telegraph*, 8 May 1935)

Fig. 2.2   Gallahers' Tobacco Factory, Belfast, May 1935 (*Belfast Telegraph*, 8 May 1935; for further discussion of women and labour, see Chap. 5 below)

to refrain from holding more meetings, passed a motion calling on the government to suppress the IUWM, Republican Congress and CPI. The UPL claimed that these groups were 'disloyal organisations and a menace to the Protestant people of Ulster'.[119] In addition, representatives of the UPL met Sir Dawson Bates to demand the suppression of republicans and leftists. In response, 'the Communist Party decided against holding public meetings which would give the pogrom organisers [sic] the opportunity to foment further trouble'.[120] The CPI claimed in May 1935 that for three Sundays in a row they had been prevented from demonstrating at the Custom House steps.[121] The following month, both the communist and ILP halls were attacked. Communists legitimately claimed this demonstrated 'the determination of the capitalist clique to foment a grand-scale pogrom if they can'.[122] The Belfast Trades Council subsequently claimed that these attacks on the communist and Labour Halls were the starting point for the subsequent sectarian violence of 1935.[123] The Trades Council claim assumes a link between anti-communist agitation and sectarian disorder. This seems reasonable given the evidence presented above from 1912 and 1920 when all those considered 'disloyal' were expelled from work in Belfast.[124]

As a result of the disorder of May 1935, Sir Dawson Bates banned all demonstrations in Belfast.[125] However, Sir Joseph Davison, Grand Master of the Orange Order, called on Orangemen to defy the ban. It was subsequently rescinded prior to the 12th of July, opening the way for the worst sectarian violence since the early 1920s. Rioting, shootings, evictions and workplace expulsions occurred during July and August 1935. Seven Protestants and three Catholics died, and over 80 people were seriously injured.[126] Evictions also caused the displacement of approximately 2500

---

[119] Inspector General's Office to Secretary, Ministry of Home Affairs, 15 May 1935 (PRONI, Ministry of Home Affairs files, HA/32/1/553).

[120] *Irish Workers' Voice*, 18 May 1935.

[121] Ibid., 25 May 1935.

[122] Ibid., 15 June 1935.

[123] Belfast and district Trades' Union Council, *Belfast and District Trades' Union Council: 1881–1951: A Short History: 70th Anniversary* (Belfast, 1951), p. 18.

[124] See the first subsection of Section II, Belfast Labour and the Politics of Sectarianism, above.

[125] L. K. Donohue, *Counter-Terrorist Law*, p. 75.

[126] A. C. Hepburn, 'The Belfast Riots of 1935', *Social History*, 15, No. 1 (Jan. 1990), 75–96 (83).

people from their homes.[127] Andrew Boyd has maintained that, in 1935, 'as at all such times, the labour organisations were powerless against the sort of sectarianism that was rampant in Belfast'.[128] A. C. Hepburn has also noted the lack of action taken by the labour movement in response to this outbreak of sectarian violence.[129]

On 13 July 1935, the *Irish Workers' Voice* reported, however, that the Belfast Trades Council had a 'heated discussion' on the topic and that the Executive had been instructed to take 'whatever steps were necessary'.[130] Similarly, CPI members met officials of the Belfast Trades Council after a week of rioting to call for 'organised working class action to meet the pogroms'.[131] The NILP and Belfast Trades Council also issued a manifesto on the strife, calling for working-class unity and a conference to be convened by the Lord Mayor to help end violence in the city.[132] As the situation worsened, left-wing individuals suffered: Tommie Geehan was evicted from his home, became the leader of the Refugees Committee on the Glenard estate, and was subsequently imprisoned for his role in organising refugees there.[133]

A. C. Hepburn and Graham Walker have contended that the first response by the labour movement was the NILP statement of 5 August 1935.[134] However, as is demonstrated above, the Belfast labour movement reacted to the sectarian violence prior to that date. Branches of the ASW and the dockers also issued labour-based appeals to end the sectarian violence.[135] As August progressed, the situation became calmer; this was exemplified at Milewater Mill where it was reported that workers faced down those trying to foment sectarian consciousness in the workplace.[136] Sections of the Belfast labour movement, including the Northern Ireland Socialist Party (NISP), CPI, and

---

[127] Hepburn gives a figure of 2241 Catholic people evicted from their homes and 64 Protestant households evicted. Therefore, a reasonable estimate of the number of Catholic and Protestant people evicted is 2500. A. C. Hepburn, 'The Belfast Riots of 1935', p. 84.

[128] Andrew Boyd, *Fermenting the Elements: The Labour Colleges in Ireland* (Belfast: Donaldson Archives, 1999), p. 76.

[129] A. C. Hepburn, 'The Belfast Riots of 1935', p. 95.

[130] *Irish Workers' Voice*, 13 July 1935.

[131] Ibid., 20 July 1935.

[132] Ibid.

[133] Ibid., 3 Aug. 1935; A. C. Hepburn, 'The Belfast Riots of 1935', pp. 86–7.

[134] A. C. Hepburn, 'The Belfast Riots of 1935', p. 77; Graham Walker, *The Politics of Frustration*, p. 95.

[135] *Irish Workers' Voice*, 10 Aug. 1935.

[136] Ibid.

Belfast Trades Council, supported the demand for a full inquiry into the reasons for sectarian unrest that summer.[137] The Belfast Trades Council also defended refugees affected by evictions,[138] sending two delegates to the British Trades Union Congress to discuss the issue.[139]

In contrast, the response of the NILP in the aftermath of the violence appears to have been fairly muted. The report of the Executive Committee of the NILP at the 1935 annual Conference, held in late September, 'regretted the recurrence of sectarian disorder in Belfast'.[140] The disorder, it argued, could only deepen divisions between workers and strengthen 'reactionary political parties'.[141] Furthermore, it asserted that if, prior to July 1935, Sir Dawson Bates had followed the recommendations placed before him by the joint NILP and Belfast Trades Council deputation, then the disorder may not have occurred.[142] Harry Midgley stated in his conference address that religion was the means by which the ruling class in Northern Ireland divided the working class and propped up social order.[143] But no concrete actions were proposed by the NILP to tackle sectarian division, discrimination or violence. Moreover, no explicit condemnation was made of the riots or those considered responsible. This lack of response suggests that the politics of sectarian violence and conflict seems to have caused sufficient division to stop a unified response by Belfast Labour.

In 1936, the NILP was forced to take a more explicit position on the issue of sectarian violence. In May of that year, the National Council for Civil Liberties (NCCL) issued a report which condemned the Special Powers Act.[144] The report was welcomed by the NILP and communists. In June 1936, members of the west Belfast Labour Party attempted to organise a campaign critical of the security policies of the Northern Ireland government.[145] A delegation of Nationalists and Labour supporters went to Westminster in the same month to lobby British MPs on religious

---

[137] Ibid., 24 Aug. 1935.
[138] Ibid., 10 Aug. 1935.
[139] Ibid., 31 Aug. 1935.
[140] Irish News, 23 Sept. 1935; Northern Whig, 23 Sept. 1935.
[141] Irish News, 23 Sept. 1935.
[142] Ibid.
[143] Ibid.
[144] NCCL, Report of a Commission of Inquiry.
[145] Inspector General's Office to Secretary, Ministry of Home Affairs, 17 and 30 June 1936 (PRONI, Ministry of Home Affairs files, HA/32/1/619).

discrimination in Northern Ireland.[146] A police report of Nationalist MP
T. J. Campbell's speech described it as 'bias[ed] and one-sided'.[147]
Exception was taken to Campbell's statements by one of the Labour del-
egation, Sam Geddis, who pointed out that sectarianism was practised by
Catholic and Protestant communities.[148] It was subsequently alleged that
the Belfast Trades Council had been represented at the meeting in
Westminster; but this was denied by the Council, which stated that it was
a 'non-sectarian body'.[149] William McMullen alluded to the contention
when he stated that 'opinion was sharply divided regarding the meeting.
He was in favour of it, but it ought not to split the trade union movement'.[150]
It was reported in the *Irish News* on 2 July 1936 that the other Labour
delegate to Westminster, NILP Councillor John Campbell, had been
intimidated out of work at the shipyard.[151] However, the police were not
convinced, claiming that:

> He [John Campbell] was not intimidated in any way, but he felt that he had
> better leave the shipyard for a time as he feared assault...There is a likeli-
> hood that Campbell may want to make political capital out of the affair.[152]

The NILP annual conference of August 1936 passed a resolution condemning the practice of expelling workers.[153] It seems remarkable that it
was 1936 before the NILP explicitly condemned workplace expulsions.
However, when the politically debilitating effects of sectarian conflict and
violence are contextualised, it becomes apparent how difficult an issue it
posed to the local labour movement.

The start of the Spanish Civil War saw the development of a spiteful
debate between Harry Midgley and supporters of the Francoist forces in
Spain. The co-operation of Belfast Labour with Irish Nationalists during
1935 and 1936 broke down as a result of left-wing sympathy for the

[146] A. C. Hepburn, 'The Belfast Riots of 1935', pp. 93–4.
[147] Inspector General's Office to Secretary, Ministry of Home Affairs, 3 July 1936 (PRONI, Cabinet files, CAB/9/B/236/2).
[148] Ibid.
[149] *Belfast Newsletter*, 3 July 1936.
[150] Ibid., 3 July 1936.
[151] *Irish News*, 2 July 1936.
[152] Inspector General's Office to Secretary, Ministry of Home Affairs, 3 July 1936 (PRONI, Cabinet files, CAB/9/B/236/2).
[153] *Irish News*, 31 Aug. 1936.

Spanish Republican Government. Significant street confrontations and intimidation occurred between Nationalists and the labour movement in Belfast during August and September 1936.[154] The NCCL secretary, Ronald Kidd, threatened to expose Irish Nationalist tactics in Belfast.[155] Harry Midgley's earnest support for the Spanish Republican government should not be doubted.[156] However, his use of strident language alienated many Catholics in Belfast. For example, his description of the Roman Catholic Church as among the powers of superstition and oppression could only have estranged Catholics.[157] Midgley's position was perceived as sectarian, although he may have merely critiqued the political positions adopted by the Roman Catholic Church. Monsignor Ryan, who debated with Midgley on the issue of Spain, claimed that Catholics were confirmed in their view of an alliance between socialists and Orangemen.[158] Midgley certainly made statements which were offensive to Catholics. As such, the perception of the stance of Midgley and his supporters as a sectarian one was reinforced by the decision of the 1937 annual conference to maintain co-operation with labour organisations in the British Commonwealth.[159]

2.3   Section III: Labour and Anti-Sectarian Politics in Belfast

To what extent was sectarian rhetoric used against the Belfast labour movement in 1924–39? First, some labour movement activists regarded themselves as politically independent from either Ulster Unionism or Irish Nationalism. Independent working-class representation was an important component of Walker and Connolly's labour politics in Belfast prior to the First World War. But this independence put the labour movement in a vulnerable position because of the ability of both Unionism and

---

[154] See 'Meetings 7 Aug. 1936–30 March 1937: Communist U[nemployed] W[orkers'] M[ovement] Friends of Soviet Russia (Part X)' (PRONI, Ministry of Home Affairs files, HA/32/1/554).

[155] Inspector General's Office to secretary, Ministry of Home Affairs, 18 Sept. 1936 (PRONI, Ministry of Home Affairs files, HA/32/1/554).

[156] Graham Walker, *The Politics of Frustration*, p. 110.

[157] Ibid., p. 96.

[158] Ibid., p. 98.

[159] For the 1937 NILP annual conference and the adoption of a new constitution by the 1938 NILP annual conference, see subsection, Belfast Labour and the Politics of Nationality, 1921–39, above.

Nationalism to deploy sectarian rhetoric against it. The UUP, in common with Nationalists and republicans, demonised the left as 'disloyal'. Any evidence of left-wing co-operation with Irish republicans was similarly utilised by the UUP government.

The religious identity of candidates could be used against the labour movement. William McMullen,[160] for example, was denounced by Nationalist opponents at the 1929 general election, and again at the by-election following Joe Devlin's death in 1934, because of his Protestant religion. Nationalists claimed that it was impossible for Catholic interests to be adequately represented by a non-Catholic. Murtagh Morgan suffered anti-Protestant rhetoric when he competed against Nationalist candidates. This occurred despite Morgan's Catholic birth.[161] It was also claimed that 'the Labour Party [in Belfast] are no friends of Catholics'.[162] Though not aimed solely at the labour movement, Sir Joseph Davison's statement in 1933 also illustrates the link of religion, politics and loyalty: 'Protestantism ... stood for Unionism, and if they found men calling themselves Protestants canvassing against the Unionists [UUP] candidate those men were traitors'.[163]

The UUP attempted to make each election a plebiscite on the border and this formed a core element of the politics of loyalty. Patrick Buckland has maintained that James Craig 'crudely tried to shift attention from bread-and-butter issues by appeals to Protestantism and loyalty'.[164] The issue of the border and the Union was not a strong issue for the left in Belfast and its opponents sought to make use of this weakness. For example, the *Belfast Telegraph* claimed, in 1925, that when the boundary was mentioned by the Labour Party, it was 'in the subject of a jest or a sneer'.[165] The *Northern Whig* stated that 'the socialists say as little as possible about the border or the maintenance of Ulster's status as an autonomous portion of the UK. They are republicans'.[166] Responding to such allegations, *The Voice of Labour* pointed out that partition was used as a 'red-herring' to

[160] NILP MP, 1925–29.
[161] Graham Walker, *The Politics of Frustration*, p. 53.
[162] *Irish News*, 10 Jan. 1930.
[163] *Belfast Newsletter*, 12 Jan. 1933.
[164] Patrick Buckland, *The Factory of Grievances: Devolved Government in Northern Ireland, 1921–39* (Dublin: Gill & Macmillan, 1979), p. 18.
[165] *Belfast Telegraph*, 31 March 1925.
[166] *Northern Whig*, 23 March 1925.

confuse the worker.[167] In 1933, a *Belfast Telegraph* editorial appealed to Loyalists on the basis that socialists were 'all silent on the question of going into a Dublin parliament'.[168] The tenuous links between the Northern Ireland and Free State Labour Parties were further used to demonstrate the suspect nature of Labour on the boundary issue. For example, the *Belfast Telegraph* argued that 'the socialists [in Northern Ireland] are closely allied to the Free State socialists who are keeping de Valera in office'.[169] The Belfast labour movement was politically vulnerable on the issue of partition. For example, Midgley and the bulk of the NILP increasingly espoused a *de facto* acceptance of partition because of their orientation towards the British labour movement. However, the CPI, SPNI and republican-socialists advocated an anti-partitionist position. In the 'zero-sum' politics of Northern Ireland, the Belfast labour movement could be accused of *both* pro-Unionism *and* 'disloyalty'. But, given the context of inter-war Belfast and Northern Ireland, the decision of the NILP to refuse a settled position on the politics of nationality was the most sensible compromise.

Religious identity formed a significant element of the Ulster Unionist and Irish Nationalist political blocs. This was expressed explicitly by Protestant and Catholic clergy influence in the mobilisation of supporters. Catholics were regularly appealed to on the basis of their religion to oppose socialism and Bolshevism. The *Irish News* and Nationalist candidates raised the issue of the atheism of socialists and the persecution of Catholics in Mexico, Spain and the USSR. The political role of the Roman Catholic Church in Belfast developed over the course of the inter-war period. For example, a relatively secular politician, like Joe Devlin, according to A. C. Hepburn, was forced to tailor his message towards the Church as a result of political developments.[170] Religious identity and politics were, however, used against the local labour movement. The inter-war context, but especially the 1930s, witnessed the deployment of sectarian rhetoric against Labour in Belfast. Furthermore, whilst the religion of candidates could be an issue, so too could religious arguments be used politically against the left.

---

[167] *The Voice of Labour*, 28 March 1925.
[168] *Belfast Telegraph*, 24 Nov. 1933.
[169] Ibid., 27 Nov. 1933.
[170] See A. C. Hepburn, *Catholic Belfast and Nationalist Ireland in the Era of Joe Devlin, 1871–1934* (Oxford: Oxford University Press, 2008).

The Ulster Unionists used religious rhetoric against the left and other common right-wing, conservative tropes of the era. It was even claimed by the *Northern Whig* that socialism was 'anti-Christian'.[171] The association of socialism, communism and atheism was used politically by both Ulster Unionism and Irish Nationalism. Nationalists at times demonised the left and Unionists as involved in a war against Catholicism: as was demonstrated by Monsignor Ryan's comment about Midgley above,[172] it was even maintained by some that socialists and extreme Protestants were involved in a conspiracy against Catholicism.[173] Religion was used occasionally as the political basis for co-operation between Unionism and Nationalism in opposition to the 'anti-Christian' threat offered by the left during the late 1920s in Belfast.[174] Similarly, in the 1930s, Dawson Bates and the Roman Catholic hierarchy, while divided politically, were united in their condemnation of communism.[175] *Both* Unionism and Nationalism, in the 1930s, opportunistically presented Labour as in league with communism.

The politics of nationality influenced the legislative construction and operation of Northern Ireland as a state. The moral economy of loyalty constructed by the UUP linked religion, nationality and ethnicity through the politico-cultural framework of loyalty and disloyalty. The existence of the NILP was an explicit recognition of the reality of a partitioned Ireland. The communists, by contrast, organised on an all-Ireland basis until the outbreak of the Second World War. Trade unions had hybrid formations depending on their history and orientation. The UULA, UTU and Ulster Workers' Trade Union all expressed the British national identity of a section of working-class people in Northern Ireland. There were no equivalent organisations amongst Irish republicans and Nationalists, although the labour movement in southern Ireland functioned in a similar way to explicitly Unionist and British working-class organisations. Consequently, Labour candidates in Belfast elections often emphasised their identification with Labour rather than a specific nationality. James Grimley, an NILP municipal candidate in the 1920s, claimed he was 'a labour representative first, last, and all the time'.[176] In contrast

[171] *Northern Whig*, 8 Jan. 1925.
[172] See the discussion of Midgley and the Spanish Civil War, above.
[173] Graham Walker, *The Politics of Frustration*, p. 52.
[174] See Chap. 3.
[175] *Irish Workers' Voice*, 7 Jan. 1933.
[176] Ibid., 12 Jan. 1925.

to those who considered themselves Labour-Unionists, Labour-Nationalists or Labour-republicans, the NILP usually stressed its non-national identification. For example, it was stated by Labour members reporting on the 1926 municipal election that 'neither prefix nor affix nor arrangement entered into the contest'.[177]

What kind of anti-sectarian rhetoric did the Belfast labour movement use during the inter-war period? The NILP was implicitly anti-sectarian because of its constitution. The founding document of the NILP called for the 'emancipation of the people' and the promotion of 'a common policy for the workers of Ireland'.[178] Similarly, the Belfast Trades Council had as its object the 'social, economic and cultural advancement of the working classes'. Communists also aimed to unite all members of the working class irrespective of race, creed or religion.[179] Explicit statements were also made against sectarianism. Tommie Geehan claimed in 1926 that the violence in 1920–22 was a result of the 'poisonous teachings and infamous dope' of the ruling class and press.[180] Geehan stated that the unity of working-class Protestants and Catholics did not suit those who fostered sectarian passions.[181] This kind of rhetoric was not confined to those on the extreme left of the labour movement, such as Geehan. Harry Midgley, for example, used anti-sectarian rhetoric. He claimed in 1934 that 'so long as you quarrel about religion you will be exploited by the landlord and the capitalist'.[182]

However, certain political issues, for example, were raised only in certain geographical areas by the NILP. For example, agitation for the release of internees in 1924 was conducted only in west Belfast and not in areas of the city identified with Unionism and Loyalism. Although Harry Midgley (in May 1924) appealed to his 'Protestant fellow-countrymen' to support the plight of interned prisoners,[183] a letter written by Robert Hill to the *Northern Whig* criticised the Gaelic Athletic Association venue of the meeting. Hill also objected to the timing of the meeting: it took place

---

[177] *The Voice of Labour*, 23 Jan. 1926.
[178] For details of the NILP founding constitution, see footnote 50 above.
[179] J. R. Campbell to members of the Belfast branch, Communist Party of Ireland, 18 Oct. 1938 (DCA, Communist Party of Ireland papers, Box 4/016).
[180] *The Voice of Labour*, 7 Aug. 1926.
[181] Ibid.
[182] Harry Midgley, *Important Facts for Old and Young* (Belfast: [no publisher details], 1934), p. 14.
[183] *The Voice of Labour*, 31 May 1924.

on a Sunday, when presumably Protestants were less likely to attend.[184] In 1933, Midgley used the pro-divorce statements of his UUP opponent to score arguably cheap political points.[185] Such statements support Rumpf and Hepburn's contention that Harry Midgley was faced with a dilemma: either be crushed by sectarian forces or manipulate them.[186] Co-operation between the left and Irish Nationalists in Britain and Ireland reinforced the perception that sections of Belfast labour were identified with one community. The NILP, however, adopted political practices associated with Second International Social-Democracy: this involved tailoring labour politics to the working class of each country.

2.3.1   Belfast Labour and the Politics of Division

There were a number of means by which the Belfast labour movement attempted to transcend sectarian division: one was to appeal to the better nature and intellect of supporters. For example, community differences were dismissed as a 'non-issue', side issue[187] or 'surface difference'.[188] In contrast, a patronising tone could be adopted as, for example, when the communist newspaper, the *Workers' Republic*, attributed the appeal of sectarian forces to 'gullible electors'.[189] To counter this, it exhorted electors to refuse to be divided on the issue of where they went to church each Sunday.[190] Slogans such as 'workers realise your responsibility' pointed to the stock which labour activists put in the more reasonable side of electors.[191] When they were successful, the NILP described their victory in glowing terms as the 'triumph of an intelligent Catholic and Protestant vote over reaction'.[192] When this appeal was unsuccessful, more derogatory language was used. Communists in the 1930s were less likely to condemn working-class people for supporting sectarian parties. Rather, they condemned the Nationalist Party and Ancient Order of Hibernians as being

---

[184] *Northern Whig*, 1 Sept. 1924.
[185] Graham Walker, *The Politics of Frustration*, p. 69.
[186] Erhard Rumpf and A. C. Hepburn, *Nationalism & Socialism*, p. 200.
[187] *Irish News*, 24 Nov. 1933.
[188] *Workers' Voice*, 19 July 1930.
[189] *Workers' Republic*, 18 Jan. 1927.
[190] Harry Midgley, *Some Important Facts for Old and Young*, p. 13.
[191] *The Voice of Labour*, 9 Jan. 1926.
[192] Ibid., 23 Jan. 1926.

as essential for imperialist rule as the UUP and Orange Order.[193] While adhering to 'third period' communism, communists were more likely to condemn 'Labour Imperialists' (Harry Midgley being depicted as the chief of this grouping) for helping the enemies of the working classes.[194]

The primary means employed by Belfast labour to transcend sectarian division were recruitment to the movement, propaganda and campaigns. Recruitment, though not explicitly designed to transcend the division, brought together those from different communities. Was the Belfast labour movement successful at transcending sectarianism during the inter-war period through recruitment? Table 2.1 details the religious background of those prominent members of the Belfast labour movement for whom we have biographical information. There are, however, only 31 people for whom we have demographic information and so the conclusions which can be drawn from the material are necessarily tentative.

The statistics indicate that the NILP was predominantly made up of people who were born Protestant and of this at least three were, or had been, members of the Orange Order or Independent Orange Order. The sample of the SPNI indicates a preponderance of Protestants. Only the communist organisations in Belfast had a close balance between those born Protestant and Catholic. Unsurprisingly, the UULA members for

Table 2.1 Religious denomination of members of the Belfast labour movement, 1918–39

Political affiliation	Protestant	Catholic
NILP	14	2
SPNI	3	1
Communist	4	3
UULA	5	0
Total	26	5

Source: D. W. Bleakley, *Saidie Patterson*, p. 12; Patrick Byrne, *The Republican Congress Revisited* (London, 1994), p. 25; *Dictionary of Irish Biography* ed. by James McGuire and James Quinn (Cambridge: Cambridge University Press, 2009) <dib.cambridge.org> [accessed: 1 May 2017]; Helga Woggon, *Winnie Carney: A Silent Radical* (no date, no place of publication), p. 1; *Irish Democrat*, 28 Aug. 1937; Austen Morgan, *Labour & Partition*, pp. 216 and 220; Graham Walker, *The Politics of Frustration*, pp. 19, 53, 59 and 83

---

[193] *Irish Workers' Voice*, 4 Nov. 1933.
[194] Ibid., 24 March 1934.

whom we have information are solely Protestant; four of these five were also Orange Order or Independent Orange Order members. The statistical evidence points to the limited cross-community appeal of the Belfast labour movement. But, it is important to note, sections of the movement were able to recruit activists from both sides of the communal division.

However, other evidence suggests that the Belfast labour movement had a wider cross-community appeal than Table 2.1 would indicate. The existence of NILP branches in both predominantly Catholic and Protestant areas points to the cross-community appeal of the party. For example, during the mid-1920s, a membership of over 200 was claimed for the Shankill Road Labour Party branch[195] and there was a vibrant Court ward Labour Party, based in the predominantly Catholic west Belfast area of the city. The Republican Congress was also able to attract Protestant members in Northern Ireland, although at the 1934 Bodenstown commemoration, the Shankill Road contingent of the Republican Congress received a hostile reception. It would be expected that the SPNI, because of its Connollyite perspective, would have had a predominantly Catholic membership, but the statistical table and other evidence suggest otherwise.

Trade union struggle and campaigns for better wages and working conditions, it was hoped, would provide a means by which sectarianism could be transcended. Although unskilled workers were more likely to be Catholic and skilled workers to be Protestant, Morgan states that ethnicity was not just an expression of 'class fractions'.[196] This is in contradistinction to Liam O'Dowd, who has claimed that 'class relations in N[orthern] I[reland] were only experienced as *sectarian class* relations'.[197] The most significant issue usually taken up by Belfast labour which did transcend sectarianism was unemployment. Loyalists co-operated with the Belfast Unemployed Committee in the early 1920s and it was from this committee that the Unemployed Workers' Organisation emerged.[198] Similarly, but on a far greater scale, Catholic and Protestant co-operation took place during the Outdoor Relief riots of 1932. The crucial point is that communists

[195] *The Voice of Labour*, 12 June 1926.

[196] Austen Morgan, *Labour & Partition*, p. 10.

[197] Liam O'Dowd, 'Shaping and Reshaping the Orange State: An Introductory Analysis', in *Northern Ireland: Between Civil Rights and Civil War* ed. by Liam O'Dowd and Mike Tomlinson (London: CSE Books, 1980), pp. 1–29 (p. 25).

[198] Christopher Norton, 'The Left in Northern Ireland 1921–32', *Labour History Review*, 40, No. 1 (1995), 3–20 (4–5).

and members of the Belfast labour movement were proved correct: working-class Protestants and Catholics could be united on an economic demand. This co-operation contradicted the propaganda of both Unionism and Nationalism. The unemployed movements in Belfast point to the potential ability of economic issues to unite working-class people in the city, and the Outdoor Relief riots in 1932 are a specific example of the realisation of such potential. However, they do not prove beyond doubt the ability of the Belfast labour movement to transcend sectarian division.

Religious belief played a role in the development of a number of labour activists. Robert Dorman, a Quaker described as having an evangelical style, quoted freely from the Bible when making political speeches.[199] Saidie Patterson, an important trade union and political activist, was a lifelong Methodist.[200] There were also a small number of Protestant Ministers in Belfast, such as the Reverend A. L. Agnew and the Reverend J. Bruce Wallace. These ministers had left-sympathising congregations and preached a Protestant Christianity informed by socialism. The association of Belfast labour with Protestantism was thus not just incidental. There does seem to have been a link, as in Britain, between dissenting Protestantism and left-wing politics.[201] Austen Morgan, for example, has claimed that in the 1950s a 'Protestant sabbatarianism' asserted itself in the NILP.[202] Aspects of this post–Second World War development of the NILP can be evinced in the practice of the inter-war NILP. There was also a current of Social-Catholicism, associated in the NILP with Patrick Agnew in Armagh,[203] and activists in the Catholic Church pre-empted the

[199] *Irish Democrat*, 28 Aug. 1937.

[200] David Bleakley, *Saidie Patterson*, p. 12.

[201] Hugh McLeod, *Religion and Society in England, 1850–1914* (Basingstoke: Palgrave Macmillan, 1996), pp. 119–21; Duncan Tanner, 'Ideological Debate in Edwardian Labour Politics: Radicalism, Revisionism and Socialism', in *Currents of Radicalism: Popular Radicalism, Organised Labour and Party Politics in Britain, 1850–1914* ed. by E. F. Biagini and A. J. Reid (Cambridge: Cambridge University Press, 1991), pp. 271–93 (pp. 289–90); for a comprehensive introduction to the relationship of the labour movement and religion in Europe, see Patrick Pasture, 'The Role of Religion in Social and Labour History', in *Class and Other Identities: Gender, Religion and Ethnicity in the Writing of European Labour History* ed. by Lex Heerma van Voss and Marcel van der Linden (Oxford: Berghan Books, 2002), pp. 101–32.

[202] Austen Morgan, *Labour & Partition*, p. 324.

[203] Aaron Edwards, *The Northern Ireland Labour Party*, p. 23.

formation of such a current in Belfast.[204] Rather, it seems, those from a Catholic background who became activists in Belfast labour, like Murtagh Morgan and Tommie Geehan, adopted a secular, communist or republican approach. However, the association of Protestant teachings with labour politics could have played a role in alienating those who considered themselves Catholic from the local labour movement.

[204] See M. N. Harris, 'Catholicism, Nationalism and the Labour Question', *Bullán*, 3, No. 1 (1997), 15–32.

CHAPTER 3

Building the 'Great March' of Progress

Abstract This chapter utilises quantitative and qualitative methods to examine the electoral performance of Labour in Belfast, at parliamentary and local government levels, in 1921–39. The party never had more than a single-figure level of councillors on Belfast Corporation or more than three MPs in the Northern Ireland parliament. This vote, however, was significantly under-represented because of the 'winner takes all' nature of simple plurality voting. Ultimately, it was questionable electoral practice and the political dominance exercised by the Ulster Unionist Party which prevented the development of a coherent Labour political voice in Belfast. The power-holders of the local regime established a plebiscitary democracy and this contributed to the lack of development of wider labour and class politics.

Keywords Northern Ireland Labour Party • Belfast • Elections

> *Labour was marching on—(cheers)—and the time was not far distant*
> *when they would follow in the footsteps of those who had achieved such a*
> *smashing victory for Labour across the water. (Cheers). It would be a*
> *disgrace to the great industrial city of Belfast if the workers lagged*
> *behind in the great march of progress. (Cheers).*
> Robert Dorman, 16 January 1924, speaking on behalf of the
> management committee of victorious Labour municipal candidate
> Clarke Scott.[1]

[1] *Irish News*, 16 Jan. 1924.

© The Author(s) 2018   67
C. J. V. Loughlin, *Labour and the Politics of Disloyalty in Belfast,*
1921–39, https://doi.org/10.1007/978-3-319-71081-5_3

By 1924, the Troubles had ended in Ireland and the two states created by partition were no longer beset by serious disorder. The Labour Party in the Irish Free State was playing an important role in the new parliament and state.[2] The British Labour Party formed its first government, albeit a minority one, in January 1924. It therefore seemed a reasonable expectation that when the Northern Ireland Labour Party (NILP)[3] was founded in 1924, it might become the main opposition to the Ulster Unionist Party (UUP) within Northern Ireland. Belfast by this time had an established record of independent labour representation. The first candidate, essentially a 'Liberal-Labour' candidate, was Alexander Bowman, who stood for North Belfast at the 1885 general election. This chapter examines the electoral politics of the precursors to the NILP and the NILP itself in Belfast in 1920–39. It utilises newspaper reports and government statistics to examine the electoral areas in Belfast which voted for the NILP at parliamentary and local government levels. The precursor to the NILP gained 12 councillors in 1920, but the NILP itself never had more than a single-figure level of councillors on Belfast Corporation, or more than three MPs in the Northern Ireland parliament, before 1939. Yet the continued existence and modest electoral returns of the NILP are evidence of a degree of political success. The evidence below will demonstrate how Labour's electoral politics in Belfast was expressed through the peculiar Northern Ireland regime.

There was some optimism in the 1920s that social and economic topics would predominate local politics.[4] However, the NILP never achieved the success it anticipated and the reasons for this failure have vexed academics. The academic consensus on the NILP, the political labour movement and wider class politics is that it failed. A major reason for the NILP's failure, it has been argued, was its inability to develop a stance on the national question in Northern Ireland.[5] Consequently, the party was subject to

---

[2] For the most comprehensive academic treatment of the Irish Labour Party, see Niámh Puirséil, *The Irish Labour Party, 1922–73* (Dublin: University College Dublin Press, 2007).

[3] The official name of the organisation was the Labour Party (Northern Ireland), but for ease of reference, the Northern Ireland Labour Party (NILP) will be the preferred title throughout these case studies.

[4] Brian Barton, 'Northern Ireland, 1921–5', in *A New History of Ireland*, 9 vols. (Oxford: Clarendon Press, 2003), *VII: Ireland 1921–84*, ed. by J. R. Hill, pp. 161–98 (pp. 162–3); Patrick Buckland, *A History of Northern Ireland* (Dublin: Gill & Macmillan, 1981).

[5] From 1924 to 1949, the NILP had no official position on the constitutional status of Northern Ireland. In 1949, the party officially accepted the constitutional position of the state. For detailed discussion of these issues, see Chap. 2.

pressure from both sides of the communal divide.[6] Linked to this was the failure to identify a strategy for building the labour movement in an ethnically divided society.[7] However, the importance of the constitutional question and communal identity does not fully explain the failure of the NILP. Another factor identified to explain failure was the changing electoral system.[8] Pringle saw the abolition of Single Transferable Vote (STV) proportional representation for Northern Ireland parliamentary elections in 1929 as aimed primarily at undermining support for independent Unionists and the NILP rather than Irish Nationalists or republicans.[9] Budge and O'Leary have also interpreted abolition of STV proportional representation for local elections as making it harder for smaller parties to get elected.[10] Social welfare reforms brought in by the Northern Ireland government are explained as another contributory factor for the NILP's failure to become the major opposition party. The UUP adoption of a 'step-by-step' policy in line with British social welfare, it is thought, hurt the NILP because it convinced 'the Protestant working-class electorate that there was no need to vote for the NILP to bring socially progressive legislation to Ulster'.[11] Only Norton and Edwards have questioned the extent of failure.[12] For example, Edwards has identified voter apathy as a reason for electoral failure.[13] This chapter will exhibit some evidence which corroborates the Norton and Edwards' view of the NILP.

[6] Patrick Buckland, *A History of Northern Ireland* (Dublin: Gill & Macmillan, 1981), p. 57; Graham Walker, *Intimate Strangers: Political and Cultural Interaction Between Scotland and Ulster in Modern Times* (Edinburgh: John Donald, 1995), p. 137; Graham Walker, 'The Northern Ireland Labour Party, 1924–45', in *Politics and the Irish Working Class, 1830–1945* ed. by Donal Ó Drisceoil and Fintan Lane (Basingstoke: Palgrave Macmillan, 2005), pp. 229–45 (p. 243).

[7] Aaron Edwards, *A History of the Northern Ireland Labour Party*, pp. 10–11.

[8] Proportional representation was used for one local election in Belfast in 1920 and two elections to the Northern Ireland parliament in 1921 and 1925; it was replaced by simple plurality vote in 1922 and 1929, respectively. See Chap. 1, footnote 46.

[9] D. G. Pringle, 'Electoral Systems and Political Manipulation: A Case Study of Northern Ireland in the 1920s', *The Economic and Social Review*, 11, No. 11 (1980), 187–205 (188 and 194).

[10] Ian Budge and Cornelius O'Leary, *Belfast: Approach to Crisis: A Study of Belfast Politics, 1613–1970* (London: Macmillan, 1973), p. 195.

[11] Graham Walker, 'The Northern Ireland Labour Party', p. 235.

[12] Aaron Edwards, *Northern Ireland Labour Party*, p. 24; Christopher Norton, 'The left in Northern Ireland 1921–32', *Labour History Review*, 40, part one (1995), 3–20 (15).

[13] Aaron Edwards, *Northern Ireland Labour Party*, pp. 16–17.

The analysis presented below is divided into three sections to answer two separate but related questions. First, how successful was Labour (and precursors) electorally in Belfast in 1920–39? To make the analysis feasible, only elections to the Belfast Corporation and for Belfast constituencies for the Northern Ireland parliament will be examined. Second, how did the NILP's vote (and precursors) develop in 1920–39? Through an examination of the electoral areas which voted for the NILP, a greater understanding of that political party will be possible. The methodology employed draws on political science, history and historical sociology. Via newspaper reports and government statistics, it has been possible to construct a profile of the electoral areas which voted NILP. However, the available statistical information is quite limited, and this is especially the case with socio-economic variables which are largely confined to housing statistics and the rateable valuation of geographical areas. Nevertheless, the use of these statistics, along with newspaper reports and NILP primary source material, has allowed a partial picture of that organisation's electoral fortunes to be built up. The image that emerges is a party which gained a sizable, but small, vote continually in Belfast. This vote, however, was significantly under-represented because of the 'winner takes all' nature of simple plurality voting. Ultimately, it was questionable electoral practice and the political dominance exercised by the UUP which prevented the development of a coherent Labour political voice in Belfast. The power-holders of the local regime ultimately established a plebiscitary democracy and this contributed to the lack of development of both Labour and wider class politics.

3.1   Section I: A Party of Trade Unionists and Workers

As a result of the Government of Ireland Act of 1920, the Northern Ireland parliament used the STV method of proportional representation for election to the region's House of Commons. The UUP administration of Northern Ireland reverted to simple plurality voting, however, for the 1929 general election. This was justified on the basis that STV was undemocratic and un-British.[14] The 1921 general election was held on Empire Day, 24 May 1921, during a period of severe polarisation, and four

---

[14] John McGarry and Brendan O'Leary, *The Politics of Antagonism: Understanding Northern Ireland* (second ed., London: Athlone Press, 1997), p. 121.

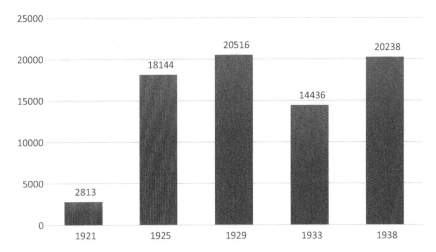

Fig. 3.1 Absolute number of votes received by Labour candidates (Independent Labour and Belfast Labour Party, 1921; NILP candidates from 1925–38) in Belfast constituencies for Northern Ireland parliamentary elections, 1921–38. (First preference votes in 1921 and 1925; simple plurality votes for 1929, 1933 and 1938.) Source: Adapted from Sydney Elliott, *Northern Irish parliamentary election results: 1921–72* (Chichester: Political Reference Publications, 1973), pp. 2–9 (pp. 89–91)

unofficial Labour candidates in Belfast received an abysmal 2813 first preference votes on an 88% turnout of the electorate (Fig. 3.1).[15]

The 1925 general election, however, was a breakthrough for the NILP as three MPs were returned for Belfast constituencies. The introduction of a simple plurality electoral system in 1929, however, acted to the detriment of the party in Belfast at the next election.[16] The vote for the NILP in Belfast at the 1929 election went up by 1%, over 2000 more votes, yet the party lost two MPs.[17] Independent Unionists were similarly

[15] Labour candidates had to stop campaigning in 1921 after Loyalists stormed an election meeting held in the Ulster Hall. See Sydney Elliott, *Northern Irish Parliamentary Election Results*, pp. 2–9; Austen Morgan, *Labour and Partition: The Belfast Working Class, 1905–23* (London: Pluto Press, 1991), pp. 263–4.

[16] For the Northern Ireland parliamentary franchise, which had had first a three-year and then a seven-year residency qualification and a company vote, see *Ulster Year Book 1929*, p. 219; *Ulster Year Book 1935*, p. 279. See Chap. 1, footnote 46.

[17] The NILP vote expanded despite a decline of nearly 100,000 electors voting.

disadvantaged. In 1925, the independent Unionists received 9% of all votes cast, returning four MPs across Northern Ireland, but in 1929, 14% of the vote saw only three MPs elected.[18] In contradistinction to this, the Nationalist vote declined in relative terms but their number of seats remained at 11.[19] This evidence concurs with D. G. Pringle's contention that the aim of abolition of STV in Northern Ireland parliamentary elections was to eliminate forms of class-based opposition from within and outside the UUP.[20]

Nine individuals stood for election to the Northern Ireland parliament for the NILP during the years of 1925 to 1938. Only Jack Beattie stood in all four elections, although he stood as an independent Labour candidate in 1938 (as a result of his expulsion from the NILP in 1934 for refusing to move the writ for Joe Devlin's old seat in west Belfast).[21] Jack Beattie was the only Labour candidate to be elected every time he stood for election to the Northern Ireland parliament during the inter-war period. Sam Kyle, William McMullen, and Harry Midgley each stood twice for the party but were elected only once. All the candidates who stood for the NILP were male, and of those whose religion can be identified, six came from a Protestant background. All four MPs who were successfully elected from Belfast in the inter-war period were from Protestant backgrounds.[22] It was claimed by contemporaries that no NILP representatives were Catholic.[23] The balance of the religious origins of members of the NILP does point towards an over-representation of Protestants and this may have lessened the appeal of that party. The evidence presented below, however, does not suggest it was a particularly significant factor in Catholic attitudes to the NILP. Gender, as well as religion, may have affected the NILP's political support. For example, following the extension of the franchise by the 1918 and 1928 Representation of the People Acts, the NILP did not stand female candidates for parliament.[24] Locally,

[18] Sydney Elliott, *Northern Irish Election Results*, pp. 89–90.

[19] Ibid.

[20] D. G. Pringle, 'Electoral Systems and Political Manipulation', p. 204.

[21] Michael Farrell, *Northern Ireland: The Orange State* (second ed., London: Pluto Press, 1980), p. 146.

[22] Patrick Buckland, *The Factory of Grievances: Devolved Government in Northern Ireland, 1921–39* (Dublin: Gill and Macmillan, 1979), p. 29.

[23] NILP candidates from a Catholic background for municipal elections, such as Murtagh Morgan and James Grimley. *Irish News*, 11 Jan. 1927.

[24] For further consideration of women, labour and politics, see Chap. 5 below.

Table 3.1   Occupational categories for Labour (NILP and independent Labour counted together) and opposition Northern Ireland parliamentary candidates for Belfast constituencies, 1921–38

Occupation	NILP	UUP	Independent Unionists	Nationalists
Trade union official	12	0	0	0
Government official	0	3	0	0
Retired military and gentleman	0	4	1	0
Law	0	3	0	1
Businessman	0	15	5	9
Worker	6	6	0	3
Other/not given	1	3	0	2
Total	19	34	6	15

Source: Nomination papers as printed in various editions of *Belfast Newsletter*, *Belfast Telegraph*, *Irish News*, and *Northern Whig*, 1925–38

only the UUP had female MPs in 1921–39, although even here this was confined to just three women MPs in Northern Ireland in 1921–39. What was the occupational status of candidates for the NILP?

In Table 3.1, 'occupational status' was that given by the candidate on their nomination paper. Given the political basis of the NILP, it is unsurprising that 'trade union official' and 'worker' were the only two categories recorded by NILP candidates. It is clear that the NILP had the largest proportion of candidates who claimed to be workers. The number of workers can be assumed to have been a positive for a party which made its appeal on the basis of, and campaigned as, a Labour Party (Fig. 3.2).

In 1920 and 1926, the party's municipal vote recorded its absolute peak. In 1920, 12 labour-supporting councillors were returned and this was reasonable given the significant number of votes garnered across the city. This is also partly accounted for by the NILP standing 10 candidates at the 1926 election, the largest number for any year excluding 1920. However, the NILP in the mid-1920s developed further political momentum following the election of five NILP Guardians to the Belfast Poor Law Board in 1924 and three MPs to the Northern Ireland parliament in 1925.[25] The 1920s saw the climax of the NILP in terms of both votes received and number of candidates. In contrast, the 1930s witnessed a decline in the party's municipal vote and number of candidates. Analysis of the NILP's vote demonstrates that Labour was systematically

[25] Christopher Norton, 'The Left in Northern Ireland', p. 7.

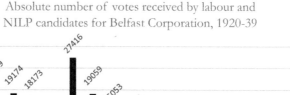

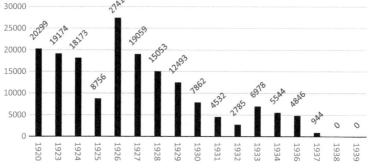

Absolute number of votes received by labour and
NILP candidates for Belfast Corporation, 1920-39

Fig. 3.2   Absolute number of votes received by NILP candidates in Belfast Corporation elections, 1920–39. Source: Adapted from Ian Budge and Cornelius O'Leary, *Belfast: approach to crisis*, p. 189; various editions of *Belfast Newsletter*, *Belfast Telegraph*, *Irish News*, and *Northern Whig*, 1924–39

under-represented by the electoral system constructed by the UUP. For example, in 1923 and 1924, Labour maintained a significant vote but was reduced from 12 labour-associated councillors to just two. Similarly, the party increased its vote in Belfast in 1929 but returned two fewer MPs. But what was the occupational category of municipal candidates who stood for Belfast Labour? (Table 3.2)

Again, these occupational classifications are based on the candidate's nomination form. The number of candidates for Labour who were trade union officials, more than half, is significant. Businessmen were over-represented in both Ulster Unionism and Irish Nationalism. Thirty-three per cent of NILP candidates were workers as compared with 18% for the UUP, whilst 25% of Nationalist candidates were workers and the rest businessmen. It can therefore be safely concluded that the vast majority of NILP candidates were workers and trade union officials. The dominance of trade unions by socialists was an issue of political concern at the time, especially in the wake of the 1926 General Strike in Britain and the Trade Disputes Act of 1927.[26] For example, during the 1927 municipal cam-

[26] The 1927 Trade Disputes and Trade Union Act was a response to the 1926 general strike, and the legislation was replicated by the Northern Irish parliament. The Act made sympathetic strike action illegal, forced civil service unions to disaffiliate from the Trades

Table 3.2   Occupational categories of NILP and opposition municipal candidates in Belfast, 1920–39

Occupation	NILP	UUP	Independent Unionists	Nationalists
Trade union official	50	2	0	0
Government official	2	1	0	0
Retired Military and Gentleman	0	2	0	0
Law	1	5	0	0
Businessman	5	65	1	12
Worker	25	18	8	4
Not given and other	4	7	1	0
Total	87	100	10	16

Source: Nomination papers as printed in various editions of *Belfast Newsletter, Belfast Telegraph, Irish News*, and *Northern Whig*, 1920–39

paign, UUP Senator W. J. McDowell commented: 'The socialist administration of trades union funds give 75 to 85 per cent of the workers' contributions to feed officials, but the out-of-work man got a very small moiety'.[27] Similarly, Joseph Cunningham, a UUP candidate in Dock ward in 1934, claimed that 'today…trades unions were monopolised by socialists, who saw to it that they were well paid for holding executive positions'.[28] As was noted above in relation to Northern Ireland parliamentary elections, the NILP ran few female candidates. Similarly, the NILP stood only two women candidates to Belfast Corporation during the inter-war period: Margaret T. McCoubrey and Ida Boyd. However, the NILP was not unique with respect to its lack of women candidates. The UUP was the only organisation which fielded female candidates against Labour: four different women between 1920 and 1939.

Naturally, owing to their differing social basis, NILP candidates disparaged the business and political backgrounds of opposition candidates.[29] Labour candidates pointed to the salaries being paid to Northern Ireland MPs and government ministers. For example, a leaflet from the Dock ward in 1929 detailed how eight UUP members and appointees of the

Union Congress, and meant trade unionists had to 'contract in' to trade union political levies rather than 'contract out' as previously. For discussion of this act and the local labour movement, see Chap. 4 below.

[27] *Northern Whig*, 12 Jan. 1927.
[28] Ibid., 11 Jan. 1934.
[29] *Belfast Newsletter*, 14 Jan. 1925.

local administration received over £1000 each from their employment. These salaries were contrasted with the ignominy of the Court of Referees, where those seeking help were shamed as 'Not genuinely seeking work'. The NILP was criticised by Unionists for attempting to stir up class conflict. Alderman Duff of the UUP, for example, stated that 'It [Jack Beattie's] was a policy of class war based on class hatred'.[30] These Unionist claims reflected contemporary fears that the working class in Belfast would be attracted to socialism.[31] It also reflected the class interests of UUP candidates who argued that rates should be kept low and Belfast Corporation run on business lines. McKinney, for example, stated in the 1924 municipal contest in Duncairn ward that 'what they wanted was businessmen to run the Corporation in a business way'.[32] Both Unionist and Nationalist organisations were dominated by businessmen. To counteract such over-representation, the Ulster Unionist Labour Association (UULA) was used as a means to demonstrate UUP concern for working-class issues. Nationalist assertions that 'the Catholics of Belfast were never enemies, but always the friends of labour'[33] should be viewed in a similar light (Table 3.3).

As can be seen above, the use of proportional representation made the 1920 Belfast Corporation election the most competitive throughout the inter-war period. The decision to implement simple plurality caused the decline of municipal electoral competition. In the 1920s, it did not stifle electoral competition, but by the end of the 1930s, it had caused the effective end of significant local municipal electoral politics. The NILP competed, during the inter-war period, most often against first, the UUP, then Nationalists, and, finally, independent Unionists. This was because the UUP held the dominant municipal position in Belfast. The peak of labour municipal electoral activity in the city occurred in 1920 and in the mid to late 1920s, a period which overlapped with its electoral success at the 1925 Northern Ireland general election. The vast majority of unopposed seats went to the UUP: 85% of seats unopposed across 1920–39.[34] This distorted the political makeup of the Corporation but also demonstrated a lack of engagement by the electorate. In the aftermath of the January

[30] *Belfast Telegraph*, 10 May 1929.
[31] Patrick Buckland, *Factory of Grievances*, p. 14.
[32] *Belfast Newsletter*, 12 Jan. 1924.
[33] *Irish News*, 8 Jan. 1929.
[34] Ian Budge and Cornelius O'Leary, *Belfast: Approach to Crisis*, pp. 186–7.

Table 3.3   Seats eligible for election, seats won unopposed, and the political affiliation of candidates in competitive Belfast municipal elections, 1920–39

Year	Seats available	Seats won unopposed	Candidates for competitive elections			
			Labour	UUP	Independent Unionists	Nationalists
1920	60	0	22	55	5	27
1923	60	21	7	27	10	17
1924	15	5	7	10	3	0
1925	15	11	4	2	0	2
1926	22	10	10	10	2	3
1927	14	6	8	7	0	1
1928	16	10	6	4	0	2
1929	23	16	5	5	2	2
1930	15	11	4	1	0	3
1931	15	13	2	3	1	0
1932	22	19	2	2	0	0
1933	15	10	6	5	2	0
1934	15	13	2	2	0	0
1936	23	17	5	2	3	2
1937	15	12	1	3	2	0
1938	15	12	0	3	3	0
1939	22	21	0	1	1	0

Source: Adapted from Budge and O'Leary, *Belfast: Approach to Crisis*, p. 179; various editions of *Belfast Newsletter*, *Belfast Telegraph*, *Irish News*, and *Northern Whig*, 1924–39; Austen Morgan, *Labour and Partition: The Belfast Working Class, 1905–23* (London: Pluto Press, 1991), pp. 257–8

1926 municipal election, NILP activists claimed they would have won four seats if STV proportional representation had still been in place, as against the one seat they actually won.[35] This contention is supported by Budge and O'Leary's evidence that the NILP consistently received fewer seats than the proportion of votes should have entitled them.[36] Unopposed returns also distorted the makeup of the Northern Ireland parliament. For example, at the 1933 general election, the UUP had a majority of seats, through unopposed returns to Stormont, before any votes had been cast. In both 1922 and 1929, it was the UUP administration which took sole responsibility for re-drawing ward boundaries for local elections.[37] The

[35] *The Voice of Labour*, 23 Jan. 1926.
[36] Ian Budge and Cornelius O'Leary, *Belfast: Approach to Crisis*, p. 191.
[37] See Patrick Buckland, *The Factory of Grievances*, pp. 236–43.

powers which the Northern Ireland administration adopted amounted to control of the political rules of the game. An essentially plebiscitary democracy, or majoritarian democracy, had been consolidated in Northern Ireland. But what can be said about the wards and areas in Belfast which voted for the NILP, in particular, in 1924–39?

3.2   SECTION II: THE 'RED' WARDS OF BELFAST, 1924–39

The next section of the chapter shifts analysis to the wards where the NILP, in particular, stood for election to Belfast Corporation in 1924–39. Table 3.4 demonstrates that the NILP competed predominantly in a small number of wards: Dock and Court wards respectively. It should be noted that the cost of competing in municipal and Northern Ireland parliamentary elections was a constant financial strain on the NILP. The Northern Ireland Senate amended the 1922 local election bill's provision of a deposit to £25, a figure which was considered prohibitive and which the UULA MP Thompson Donald protested against at the time.[38] This was compounded by the introduction of the 1927 Trade Disputes Act.[39] Reproduced below Table 3.4 is a map of the 15 wards of Belfast: the shaded areas represent wards where the NILP stood more than five times. NILP electoral campaigns were confined mostly to the central and western parts of the city. What is also notable is that these wards varied significantly in size and contrast unfavourably with the nine, proportionally equal, wards which had been utilised at the 1920 municipal election (Fig. 3.3).

Two types of ward have been identified and grouped together to analyse the vote for the NILP in Belfast in 1924–39: a 'successful' group and an 'unsuccessful' group. The 'successful' group of wards has been identified on the basis that the NILP stood for election there four or more times and was elected two or more times during 1924–39; it is made up of Court, Dock, St. George's, and Smithfield wards. The 'unsuccessful' group has been identified on the basis that the NILP stood for election in these wards four or more times and was never elected or was elected only once in 1924–39; it is made up of Clifton, Falls, Shankill, and Woodvale wards. The wards which have been categorised in the 'successful' and

---

[38] *Hansard N.I. (Commons)*, ii, 917 (5 July 1922).

[39] Northern Ireland Labour Party, *Report of Executive Committee to 5th Annual Conference, 31 Mar. 1928* (Belfast, 1928), pp. 2–3.

Table 3.4 Belfast municipal wards where the NILP stood and number of wins, 1924–39

Ward	Number of times stood	Number of wins[a]
Dock	13	9
Court	9	3
Smithfield	7	2
Falls	6	1
St. George's	5	3
Clifton	5	0
Pottinger	4	0
Shankill	4	0
Woodvale	4	0
Cromac	3	0
Victoria	2	0
Duncairn	1	0
Ormeau	1	0
St. Anne's	1	0
Windsor	0	0

Source: Various editions of *Belfast Newsletter*, *Belfast Telegraph*, *Irish News*, and *Northern Whig*, 1924–39

[a]Excludes unopposed wins

'unsuccessful' groups account for 82% of the attempts at election made by the NILP to Belfast Corporation.

From Table 3.5, it is apparent that the wards in the 'successful' group are smaller, in terms of both population and the electorate, than the Belfast mean and the 'unsuccessful' group. In terms of population size, only Clifton and Falls grew in absolute numbers; it appears that the NILP may have been more likely to compete in wards in population decline. In terms of electorate, the 'successful' group is essentially static, apart from a substantial decline in Smithfield ward, whereas two wards, Clifton and Falls, in the 'unsuccessful' group saw a substantial increase in electorate. These figures are important because between 1926 and 1938 the total population of the Belfast Corporation area rose by 22,935 persons[40] while the electorate increased by 17,358 persons.[41]

Given the relationship in Belfast between politics, religion and ethnicity, the confessional balance of the wards is a significant variable.[42]

[40] *Census of Population of Northern Ireland 1937*, p. 15.

[41] *Ulster Year Book 1926* (Belfast: HMSO, 1927), p. 141; *Ulster Year Book 1938* (Belfast: HMSO), p. 315.

[42] For discussion of labour, nationalism and sectarianism, see Chap. 2.

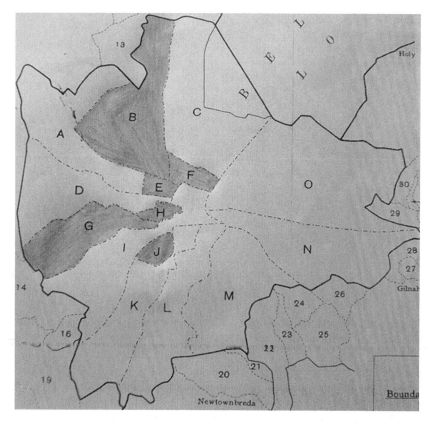

Fig. 3.3   Map of electoral wards of Belfast Corporation. (*Census of population of Northern Ireland 1951: general report* (Belfast, 1955), appendix). Key: A, Shankill; B, Clifton; C, Duncairn; D, Woodvale; E, Court; F, Dock; G, Falls; H, Smithfield; I, St. Anne's; J, St. George's; K, Windsor; L, Cromac; M, Ormeau; N, Pottinger; O, Victoria. Shaded areas represent wards where the NILP stood for municipal election five times or more, 1924–39

Newspapers at the time claimed that Catholics were likely to vote NILP.[43] Table 3.6 demonstrates that wards where the NILP won three or more competitive elections to Belfast Corporation were not demographically

[43] *Belfast Newsletter*, 16 Jan. 1925, 16 Jan. 1926, and 15 Nov. 1933; *Belfast Telegraph*, 2 April 1925, 6 and 14 Jan. 1928, 8 Jan. 1929, 17 and 24 May 1929; *Northern Whig*, 8 Jan. 1925, 10 and 17 Jan. 1927, 9 Jan. 1928; *Irish News*, 14 Jan. 1925, 16 Jan. 1926, 9 and 17 Jan. 1928, 11 Jan. 1929, 7 Jan. 1930, and 29 Nov. 1933.

Table 3.5   Population and electorate for selected wards of Belfast Corporation, 1926 and 1937, where the NILP stood 'successfully' and 'unsuccessfully', 1924–39

Ward	Population		Electorate	
	1926	*1937*	*1926*	*1937*
'Successful' wards				
Court	20,218	17,698	8259	8297
Dock	20,970	17,473	7258	7705
St. George's	18,974[a]	15,770	6883	6643
Smithfield	12,637	10,840[b]	6162	5280
Mean 'successful' wards	18,200	15,445	7141	6981
'Unsuccessful' wards				
Clifton	34,501	46,584[c]	13,303	17,018
Falls	29,604	31,746[d]	11,313	12,728
Shankill	35,654[e]	33,298	14,205	14,767
Woodvale	25,516	23,777[f]	11,536	11,342
Mean 'unsuccessful' wards	31,319	33,851	12,589	13,963
Mean all Belfast wards	26,677	29,206	12,065	13,259

Source: *Census of Population of Northern Ireland 1926: Belfast Country Borough* (Belfast: His Majesty's Stationery Office, 1927), pp. 2 and 26; *Census of Population of Northern Ireland 1937: Belfast Country Borough* (Belfast: HMSO, 1937), pp. 2 and 31; various editions of *Belfast Newsletter, Belfast Telegraph, Irish News,* and *Northern Whig*, 1924–39; *Ulster Year Book 1929* (Belfast: His Majesty's Stationery Office, 1929), p. 226; *Ulster Year Book 1938,* (Belfast: HMSO, 1938), p. 315

[a]1927
[b]1936
[c]1936
[d]1936
[e]1927
[f]1928

exclusively Catholic. Dock ward, where the NILP was municipally most successful, had a close confessional balance. Only Clifton ward is in any way comparable to Dock ward. A reason for this success may have been the ability of the party to appeal to both sides of the communal divide. Other wards in both groups, excluding Dock and Court ward, were over-whelmingly composed of one confessional group or another.

From Tables 3.7 and 3.8, it appears that the 'successful' group may have been poorer than the 'unsuccessful' group. This is due to the rate-able valuation of the latter group being significantly higher than the for-mer. However, the 'unsuccessful' group was larger geographically and in terms of population, so the more comparable statistic to use is rateable

Table 3.6 Religious composition of selected wards of Belfast Corporation, 1926 and 1937, where the NILP stood 'successfully' and 'unsuccessfully', 1924–39

Ward	Religion (%)			
	Catholic		Protestant[a]	
	1926	1937	1926	1937
'Successful' wards				
Court	23	25	66	69
Dock	42	45	45	46
St. George's	5	4	82	84
Smithfield	91	91	8	8
Mean 'successful' wards	35	37	54	56
'Unsuccessful' wards				
Clifton	25	30	60	57
Falls	89	92	9	7
Shankill	5	5	79	79
Woodvale	5	5	82	82
Mean 'unsuccessful' wards	30	34	58	55
Mean all Belfast wards	24	24	66	64

Source: *Census of Population of Northern Ireland: 1926*, pp. 2 and 26; *Census of Population of Northern Ireland: 1937*, pp. 2 and 31

[a]This includes only Church of Ireland and Presbyterians

Table 3.7 Rateable valuation and rateable valuation per elector for selected wards of Belfast Corporation, 1926 and 1937, where the NILP stood 'successfully' and 'unsuccessfully', 1924–39

Ward	Rateable valuation (£)		Rateable valuation per elector (£ s d)	
	1926	1937	1926	1937
'Successful' wards				
Court	39,662	54,491	4 16 0	6 11 5
Dock	59,995	79,949	8 5 5	10 7 7
St. George's	43,175	64,199	6 5 5	9 13 5
Smithfield	49,955	71,514	8 2 0	13 10 10
Mean 'successful' wards	48,197	67,538	6 17 2	10 8 0
'Unsuccessful' wards				
Clifton	1,18,547	2,19,132	8 18 2	12 17 7
Falls	61,683	98,380	5 9 0	7 14 7
Shankill	70,192	1,06,916	4 18 10	7 4 10
Woodvale	63,608	92,819	5 10 2	8 3 7
Mean 'unsuccessful' wards	78,508	1,29,312	6 4 0	9 0 0
Mean all Belfast wards	1,16,211	1,86,537	9 12 7	14 1 5

Source: *Census of Population of Northern Ireland: 1926*, pp. 2 and 26; *Census of Population of Northern Ireland: 1937*, pp. 2 and 31; *Ulster Year Book 1929*, p. 226; *Ulster Year Book 1938*, p. 315

Table 3.8   Population density and housing conditions for selected wards of Belfast Corporation, 1926 and 1937, where the NILP stood 'successfully' and 'unsuccessfully', 1924–39

Ward	Population density		People per room		Rooms per person	
	1926	1937	1926	1937	1926	1937
'Successful' wards						
Court	188.95	165.4	1.31	1.2	0.81	0.88
Dock	114.59	95.48	1.36	1.16	0.84	0.96
St. George's	141.59	117.69	1.39	1.18	0.84	0.99
Smithfield	137.36	116.56	1.48	1.29	0.72	0.81
Mean 'successful' wards	146.62	123.78	1.38	1.2	0.8	0.91
'Unsuccessful' wards						
Clifton	22.27	30.05	0.9	0.84	1.18	1.23
Falls	36.68	39.34	1.31	1.15	0.8	0.89
Shankill	25.99	24.25	1.16	0.96	0.89	1.05
Woodvale	23.85	22.22	1.22	1.01	0.84	0.99
Mean 'unsuccessful' wards	27.2	28.97	1.15	0.99	0.93	1.04
Mean all Belfast wards	28.05	28.65	1.09	0.92	0.98	1.13

Source: *Census of Population of Northern Ireland 1926*, pp. 2–8 and p. 26; *Census of Population of Northern Ireland 1937*, pp. 2–6 and p. 31; *Ulster Year Book 1929*, p. 226; *Ulster Year Book 1938*, p. 315

valuation per elector. Comparisons of these two statistics show that both groups were between three to five pounds per person poorer than the Belfast ward average for 1926 and 1937 respectively. In terms of the socio-economic class of people living in the 'successful' and 'unsuccessful' groups, we can say they were probably very similar. Rateable valuation had a significant impact on the size of the electorate as the occupant had to live in a dwelling of five pounds rateable valuation or more in order to vote.[44] The UUP government considered changing the local government franchise in 1922 but did not. In 1929, the franchise was altered for both local elections and Northern Ireland parliament elections to include a residency qualification and a business vote.[45] The role of rateable valuation helps explain why the wards in the 'unsuccessful' group had a significantly larger population than the Belfast ward average

[44] Sydney Elliott, 'The Electoral System in Northern Ireland since 1920', 2 vols. (unpublished PhD thesis, Queen's University Belfast, 1970), I, p. 262.
[45] See Chap. 1, footnote 46.

yet a negligibly larger electorate.[46] The population density of the 'successful' group is significantly higher than that of the 'unsuccessful' group. This suggests that the areas where the NILP succeeded in getting elected were more likely to be areas of overcrowding and therefore where the issue of housing was additionally acute. The statistics for people per room and rooms per person complicate the issue slightly. Both 'successful' and 'unsuccessful' groups were likely to have overcrowded houses in comparison with the Belfast ward average. The 'successful' group was, in important respects, more crowded than the 'unsuccessful' group and this fits with our population density statistic. The above statistics suggest that while both groups were similar in socio-economic status, issues of overcrowding and slum housing may have been more acute in areas where the NILP was successful electorally than in areas where they were unsuccessful.

The socio-economic variables from the above table show a marginal improvement in the level of housing between 1926 and 1937. This can be seen through the decline in the population density of the wards contained in the 'successful' group. It is also evident from the fall in people per room and the rise in the rooms per person. However, the table also shows an absolute fall of population of approximately 2000–3000 people in each ward contained in the 'successful' group. This leaves it open as to whether the improvement in the figures was due to increased levels of housing or due to falls in population. D. S. Johnson has argued that analysts of inter-war Northern Irish housing have viewed it in too negative a perspective.[47] At the level of Belfast, Johnson states that 'housing conditions while poor, were improving'.[48] The evidence presented above highlights that while this may have been true at the macro level, there were still definite pockets of worse-than-average housing conditions. This evidence fits with the economically orthodox housing policy applied by the UUP in 1921–39 and the evidence of poor and slum housing documented during the Second World War.[49]

[46] See Table 3.7 above.

[47] D. S. Johnson, 'The Northern Irish Economy, 1914–39', *An Economic History of Ulster, 1820–1939* ed. by Liam Kennedy and Philip Ollerenshaw (Manchester: Manchester University Press, 1985), pp. 184–223 (pp. 208–9).

[48] Ibid., p. 209.

[49] See relevant chapters of *Ulster since 1600: Politics, Economy and Society* ed. by Liam Kennedy and Philip Ollerenshaw (Oxford: Oxford University Press, 2013).

3.3   SECTION III: THE MUNICIPAL POLITICS
          OF THE BELFAST NILP

Now that statistical variables have been looked at and some tentative conclusions drawn, it is necessary to turn to the municipal politics of the
NILP. To gain an impression of the issues mentioned most often by candidates at elections, press reports on candidates were analysed. For each
year in 1924–39, three speeches or manifestos were analysed to identify
how often specific issues or policies were mentioned. NILP, UUP and
Irish Nationalists or independent Unionist candidates were analysed.
Eight topics were identified: housing, temperance, wages, ex-serviceman,
employment, education, identity[50] and other. The topics were chosen on
the basis that eight was a manageable number for analysis and that they
could reflect the issues raised most regularly by candidates. 'Education'
and 'other' issues developed in importance for the NILP during the 1930s:
the issue of education, for example, was raised more often every year by
Labour candidates than by opposing candidates. 'Wages' was mentioned
approximately the same number of times by all candidates, apart from in
the mid-1920s, when NILP candidates discussed it the most. Employment
was apt to be raised by candidates of all parties. 'Housing' was more
important for all candidates in the 1920s than in the 1930s. NILP candidates did not have a monopoly on the issues of wages, employment or
housing. Unionist and Nationalist organisations, as cross-class entities,
had to appeal politically through social and economic issues. It appears
that, in constituencies where the NILP competed, once the party raised
certain topics, their opponents responded in kind. Only issues of identity
seem to have been monopolised by opponents of the NILP. This concurs
with the stated aim of the party, which was to break the working class away
from the old political parties.[51] However, certain issues were not raised in
the wards analysed. The issue of temperance, for example, was scarcely
mentioned by any of the candidates considered. This is due to the sample
taken, which did not contain the wards where temperance seems to have
been an important issue.

How did the NILP present its political programme to the electorate?
According to Patrick Buckland, socialism was not a vote winner for the

[50] 'Identity' is here taken to include issues of nationality, religion and ethnicity.
[51] *The Voice of Labour*, 4 April 1925.

NILP.[52] The NILP rarely used the word 'socialist' in its election literature or during campaigning. In contrast, both the Unionist and Nationalist press used the word 'socialist' as a derogatory epithet for the NILP.[53] The NILP, however, did call for 'social and economic emancipation'.[54] This rhetoric was tempered by practical, reformist politics such as their oft-used municipal election slogan of the 1920s, 'Fair play for all, privilege for none'.[55] Despite moderate Labour rhetoric, the *Northern Whig* talked of the 'socialist viper', and the *Irish News* referred to the left as the 'spurious Socialistic-Communistic canker growth'.[56] The NILP advocated 'social ownership', which was a euphemism for socialism,[57] yet the reforms advocated by Labour candidates were modest. For example, Dawson Gordon supported all 'genuine' attempts at efficient Corporation administration in 1926. The advantage of this approach is that certain parts of the NILP's political manifesto were eminently achievable. The disadvantage was this made it easier for Ulster Unionism or Irish Nationalism to absorb the NILP's political demands. The UUP, for example, depicted itself as the party of 'progress and prosperity'.[58]

The modest nature of the NILP's political programme is further demonstrated in the issue of housing. Dawson Gordon's manifesto, in 1926, advocated that the Corporation maintain its 'duty' to keep people adequately housed and that vacant housing be compulsorily let. Clarke Scott's manifesto of 1927 for Court ward was more radical in that it called for a municipal house building programme carried out by Corporation-employed labour. Yet before the NILP had raised the issue, a UUP candidate boasted that he was responsible for the building of 200 houses in Court ward.[59] In this context, where the UUP had demonstrable power to dispose of patronage, it may have appeared to electors more profitable to support the local elite. In this sense, then, the UUP could be a better bet

[52] Patrick Buckland, *Factory of Grievances*, p. 30.

[53] *Belfast Newsletter*, 6 Jan. 1925.

[54] *Belfast Telegraph*, 16 May 1929.

[55] *Northern Whig*, 9 Jan. 1928.

[56] *Irish News*, 7 Jan. 1930; *Northern Whig*, 8 Jan. 1925.

[57] 'An Open Letter to the Electors by Alderman Harry Midgley, Parliamentary Labour Candidate for Dock', July 1932 (PRONI, Records of Sam Napier, 'An open letter to the electors by Alderman Harry Midgley, parliamentary labour candidate for Dock', p. 1, D/3702/B/4A-G).

[58] *Belfast Newsletter*, 11 Jan. 1928.

[59] *Belfast Newsletter*, 12 Jan. 1924.

for 'social reform' than the NILP. Similarly, the housing scandal, which was exposed by the Megaw Report in 1926, may have tarnished all political parties on the Corporation in the view of electors.[60]

The politics of the Belfast Corporation, as in much of Northern Ireland, were bound up with sectarianism and communal division. For the NILP, which presented its appeal on the basis of social and economic issues, communal tensions were always likely to be difficult.[61] A further complication was the ability of both Unionism and Nationalism to appeal to Labour supporters. For example, NILP supporters defected to Joe Devlin's election campaign in March 1925.[62] A related problem was convincing electors that businessmen could not represent the interests of labour. A typical example of their opponents' argument was given when the Nationalist candidate Agnew was described as the 'true friend of labour'.[63] Similarly, Sir Joseph Davison, a UULA member and UUP municipal candidate in 1933, claimed that 'the just claims of labour had always been well looked after by the Unionist members'.[64] The 'step-by-step' welfare policy of the Northern Ireland government has also been considered an impediment to the development of Labour in Northern Ireland.[65] Some in the NILP considered this a false argument as economic and social conditions were worse in the province than in Britain.[66]

The NILP in its election material for the Corporation predominantly appealed to electors on the basis of policies rather than religious affiliation or identity.[67] William McMullen, in his victory speech for the 1925 municipal election for Smithfield ward, stated that the only negative his Nationalist opponents could throw at him was that he was a Protestant.[68] The two wards considered Catholic were Smithfield and Falls, the only

---

[60] The Megaw report investigated the procurement and building of houses by the Belfast Corporation. It substantiated claims of over-payment for timber and criticised the administration of housing by Belfast Corporation and lack of supervision by the Corporation's Housing Committee. See R. D. Megaw, *Report of the Inquiry into the Housing Schemes of the Belfast Corporation* (Belfast: HMSO, 1926).

[61] See Chap. 2.

[62] *The Voice of Labour*, 28 March 1925.

[63] *Irish News*, 10 Jan. 1928.

[64] *Belfast Newsletter*, 12 Jan. 1933.

[65] Graham Walker, *A History of the Ulster Unionist Party: Protest, Pragmatism and Pessimism* (Manchester: Manchester University Press, 2004), p. 76.

[66] *The Watchword*, 20 Dec. 1930.

[67] *Irish News*, 12 Jan. 1925.

[68] Ibid., 16 Jan. 1925.

wards with Catholic majorities. Irish Nationalist politicians saw Catholicity and Nationalism as synonymous, arguing that only Catholics could represent the interests of the wards genuinely.[69] On the Ulster Unionist side, a complementary argument was made with regard to Protestantism and Unionism.[70] At the crux of this lay a conception of politics as a 'zero-sum' game. This was articulated by the *Irish News*, for example, when they talked of the Nationalists and NILP combining in an 'anti-Reactionary party' vote.[71] The paper made it clear in this editorial statement that this was a purely opportunistic political manoeuvre against the UUP, stating that 'when the issue is made one of religious party versus political party we obviously plump for the former'.[72] Nationalists also attempted to use sectarian attacks on Catholics against the NILP; for example, this argument was used against NILP candidates in 1925.[73] Similarly, it was used against Harry Midgley in the 1938 Northern Ireland general election.[74] Sectarian appeal was reinforced by the signing of nomination papers by priests, a practice replicated by the role of the Orange Order in rallying support for the UUP.[75] A. C. Hepburn has concluded that Nationalists in Belfast, following the abolition of STV for Northern Ireland parliamentary elections, 'had little choice but to retreat into the cocoon of a minority sectarian party'.[76] A further issue which affected the NILP vote was the basis on which the franchise was exercised in Belfast.

The restricted franchise for local government and abolition of STV proportional representation had a disproportionate impact upon the representation of the NILP.[77] The vote of the NILP was reasonably consistent. The occupation of a dwelling worth five pounds of rateable value to be eligible to vote, however, hurt the NILP.[78] As was seen in the above tables, the wards where the NILP stood for election, both successfully and

[69] Ibid., 9 Jan. 1925, 14 Jan. 1926, 14 Jan. 1927, and 9 Jan. 1928.

[70] *Belfast Newsletter*, 12 Jan. 1933.

[71] *Irish News*, 8 Jan. 1930.

[72] Ibid.

[73] *Irish News*, 8, 9, and 14 Jan. 1925.

[74] Graham Walker, *The Politics of Frustration*, p. 107; see Betty Sinclair's explanation for Harry Midgley's defeat at the 1938 Northern Irish general election, Chap. 2.

[75] *Belfast Newsletter*, 27 Nov. 1933; *Belfast Telegraph*, 18 Jan. 1927; *Irish News*, 10 Jan. 1928; *Northern Whig*, 12 Jan. 1927.

[76] A. C. Hepburn, *Catholic Belfast and Nationalist Ireland in the Era of Joe Devlin, 1871–1934* (Oxford: Oxford University Press, 2008), p. 264.

[77] See footnote 46, Chap. 1.

[78] Sydney Elliott, 'The Electoral System', I, p. 262.

unsuccessfully, were more likely to be poorer areas, in terms of rateable valuation, and had a lower proportion of the population eligible to vote. Budge and O'Leary have argued that 'the groups excluded from the franchise [for local government elections] may have been the ones who were most likely to vote against the dominant Unionists—Catholics in particular and possibly also the working classes'.[79] The role of company voting would also have had an impact on the NILP's electoral chances as they were unlikely to have benefitted from these business peoples' votes. It has not been possible to identify company votes on a ward basis, but figures given by Sydney Elliott show that the average number of company votes in Belfast was 1650 votes per year, and approximately a third of these votes were concentrated in wards in west Belfast.[80] Given that the NILP stood and was elected most often in the central and western wards of Belfast, it seems a reasonable supposition that this company vote may have impacted negatively on their chances of getting elected. The role of the franchise and electoral practices, therefore, contributed to the 'failure' of Belfast labour politically. A further issue was finance.

In 1922, the UUP government introduced a £25 deposit for local election candidates. This would pose a significant barrier to entry into local politics for the NILP and it reflected a wider lack of financial and organisational development of that party. Clarke Scott, speaking in the aftermath of his victory in 1924, stated that his election costs were £30.[81] Three years later, in 1927, £50 was spent successfully returning Clarke Scott for the same ward.[82] One activist bemoaned the necessity of candidates having to raise the £25 deposit and proposed a central deposit fund so that the concentration of those involved in campaigning could be focused on raising election expenses.[83] The only other year for which official financial accounts are available is 1939. The 1939 local government election fund generated just five pounds from five trade unions.[84] Harry Midgley complained in 1929 that he couldn't get trade union support and

---

[79] Ian Budge and Cornelius O'Leary, *Belfast: Approach to Crisis*, p. 178.
[80] Sydney Elliott, 'The Electoral System', II, p. 789.
[81] *Irish News*, 16 Jan. 1924.
[82] Northern Ireland Labour Party, *Organisational and Financial Report 1927–8* (Belfast, 1928), p. 7.
[83] *The Irishman*, 4 Jan. 1930.
[84] Northern Ireland Labour Party, *Report of the Executive Committee to 16th Annual Conference* (Belfast, 1939), p. 2.

so was unable to contest the Northern Ireland general election.[85] In 1938, the NILP tried to stand 11 candidates but managed only seven because of a lack of finance.[86] The NILP's inability to contest the majority of seats in Belfast also allowed official Unionists 'to concentrate party resources in marginal seats'.[87] The NILP was essentially a victim of the political rules and culture which it did not control. It would ultimately require intervention from London to change local electoral practice in the 1970s in Northern Ireland.

The major explanations that contemporaries identified for the electoral successes of the NILP were, firstly, the role of apathy amongst the electorate and, secondly, the voting preferences of Catholics. Jack Milan's election in 1924 for Dock ward, for example, was partly explained due to voter apathy.[88] Harry Midgley, it was also claimed, won the same ward due to the apathy of UUP voters in 1928.[89] Apathy was used as a generic explanation for any gains made by the NILP.[90] Domination of trade unions by socialists was similarly explained as a result of the apathy of the membership of trade unions.[91] Why apathy favoured the NILP was never explained in the editorials of newspapers; it was simply assumed that a greater turnout of the electorate would have resulted in more votes for official Ulster Unionist or Irish Nationalist candidates. The nature of Catholic political preferences was also frequently deployed to explain the success of the NILP. In particular, Catholic and Nationalist votes in Dock and Pottinger wards were highlighted as explanations for NILP success.[92] It was assumed that Catholic votes automatically went against UUP candidates. Given the nature of politics in Northern Ireland, this seems a relatively safe assumption. Yet, in Dock ward in 1926, Dawson Gordon won against the opposition of both UUP and Nationalist candidates. If Gordon had won only Catholic votes, it would have been impossible for him to win the ward. A straight fight between a Nationalist and NILP candidate in Dock ward again saw the NILP win in 1930. Similarly, purely Catholic

---

[85] Graham Walker, *The Politics of Frustration*, p. 52.

[86] *Belfast Telegraph*, 25 and 29 Jan. 1938.

[87] Ian Budge and Cornelius O'Leary, *Belfast: Approach to Crisis*, p. 177.

[88] *Northern Whig*, 16 Jan. 1924.

[89] *Belfast Telegraph*, 17 Jan. 1928.

[90] *Belfast Newsletter*, 2 Dec. 1933; *Belfast Telegraph*, 7 April 1925 and 16 Jan. 1933; *Irish News*, 15 Jan. 1930.

[91] *Belfast Telegraph*, 13 Jan. 1926.

[92] Ibid., 17 May 1929; *Belfast Newsletter*, 15 Nov. 1933; *Irish News*, 16 Jan. 1926.

support for the NILP fails to account for the party's ability to win thousands of votes in the overwhelmingly Protestant Shankill ward.[93] Secondary explanations included population increase and the role of independent Unionists in splitting the vote.[94]

The role of sectarianism could be a double-edged sword for the NILP. It was usually negative but Labour candidates did sometimes attempt to use issues associated with confessional division for their own advantage. In 1933, as a means of gaining support for the NILP, Midgley used his UUP opponent's pro-divorce stance and comments that courting couples should be allowed to make use of the grounds of Stormont.[95] Issues of nationality could also, however, be sidestepped by skilful candidates. Jack Beattie, for example, was criticised for having advocated a 'workers' republic' but responded by stating that he had been misquoted and what he said was that 'the only government likely to raise the standard of the working classes was a workers' government'.[96] However, in the sectarian atmosphere of Northern Ireland, the issue of the border, national identity, and religious persuasion was bound to cause controversy for the NILP. The key advantage the party had was its ability to appeal to both sides of the communal divide. But it was also a problem for the NILP when candidates made contradictory pronouncements on the issue of nationality. For example, this was the case when Jack MacGougan stood in Oldpark and made anti-partitionist statements.[97] Midgley, in contradistinction, was described as a 'strong partitionist'[98] by the *Irish News* after helping to defeat the pro-united Ireland 'Armagh resolution' at the NILP 1937 annual conference.[99]

The abolition of STV proportional representation was also a problem as it meant the NILP could not maintain the tactical co-operation which had developed with Irish Nationalists in 1925–29. Tactical voting benefitted

[93] In 1930, 1931, and 1933, NILP candidates received 2260, 2605, and 1450 votes in Belfast Corporation elections for the Shankill ward.
[94] *Belfast Newsletter*, 2 Dec. 1933; *Belfast Telegraph*, 24, 25 and 31 March 1925.
[95] 'Harry Midgley to the Electors of Dock Division', Nov. 1933 (PRONI, Harry Midgley Papers, D/4089/4/1/36).
[96] *Belfast Telegraph*, 25 and 26 Jan. 1925.
[97] *Irish News*, 5 Feb. 1938.
[98] Ibid., 2 Feb. 1938.
[99] The 'Armagh resolution' was a pro-Irish unity amendment moved at the NILP's 1937 annual conference. Midgley and his supporters helped defeat the motion and alternatively orientated the party towards links with the British Labour Party.

Labour politicians in Belfast at times; for example, 57% of Joe Devlin's surplus at the 1925 Northern Ireland general election went to William McMullen.[100] But tactical voting could also be deployed by Ulster Unionists and Irish Nationalists against Labour. For example, the *Northern Whig* identified NILP electoral success as necessitating an anti-socialist alliance of Unionism and Nationalism.[101] It explicitly called on Protestant voters to support Irish Nationalist candidates versus the NILP.[102] The *Belfast Telegraph* endorsed a similar though less explicit policy.[103] As stated above, historians have debated why the Northern Ireland government abolished STV proportional representation for parliamentary elections. Given Ulster Unionist demonisation of all opposition as 'wittingly and unwittingly' helping Ulster's enemies, it seems probable that abolition was carried out partly to stop the development and consolidation of a coalition against UUP rule.[104]

The issue of Catholic voters electing NILP candidates was an issue of some controversy in municipal elections. Given the constituencies in which Jack Beattie was elected to the Northern Ireland parliament (East Belfast in 1925 and from 1929 onwards Pottinger), it seems reasonable to assume that he attracted the votes of Catholic electors. However, given the religious demography of the parliamentary as well as Corporation electoral areas, it seems extremely unlikely that only Catholic electors voted for him or any other NILP candidates. The *Northern Whig* stated in 1927 that 'it is from the Roman Catholic community that the Socialists derive any backing they have in this city'.[105] The *Irish News* responded, 'there has never been a Socialist who professed himself a Catholic in a position of influence or prominence in the public life of Belfast'.[106] As noted above, there was a definite anti-UUP vote. The *Irish News* in 1933 even wrote of how a majority had voted against the UUP.[107] While a component of the NILP's parliamentary vote must have been anti-Unionist, the depth of this is hard to gauge. Given the nature of the NILP as a political organisation and the tradition of labourism, with whatever qualifications, it seems

---

[100] A. C. Hepburn, *Catholic Belfast and Nationalist Ireland*, p. 257.
[101] *Northern Whig*, 16 Jan. and 30 March 1925.
[102] *Northern Whig*, 13 and 16 Jan. 1925.
[103] *Belfast Telegraph*, 13 Jan. 1925.
[104] *Belfast Newsletter*, 16 Nov. 1933.
[105] *Northern Whig*, 10 Jan. 1927.
[106] *Irish News*, 11 Jan. 1927.
[107] *Irish News*, 17 Jan. 1933.

reasonable to see the NILP parliamentary vote as at least partly 'labourist'. The labour vote was consistent in Belfast, but hurdles to participation and elite control prevented its viable expression. When the politics of identity was in the ascendant, support for the NILP declined. Furthermore, this seems reasonable given that the vote for the NILP threatened *both* Unionists and Nationalists alike: For Unionists, Labour was 'disloyal', socialist and republican; for Nationalists, the Catholic Church and local businessmen, Labour was too secular and socialist.

3.4   CONCLUSION

The NILP and local Labour were fundamentally hindered by the decision to abolish STV proportional representation for local elections (1922) and Northern Ireland parliament elections (1929). The introduction of a business franchise, residency qualification and reversion to the 1890s local authority ward boundaries restricted local Labour representation. The majoritarian control instituted by the UUP restricted representation of all minorities. This context means that previous analysis about the failure of Labour and wider class politics should be qualified. The failure of class politics and Labour was due to the political culture created by the power-holders of Northern Ireland's society. How this politics of loyalty was constituted in some areas of legislation is examined in the next chapter.

CHAPTER 4

Labour, Law and the State in Northern Ireland, 1921–39

Abstract Utilising a case study approach, this chapter examines how two pieces of legislation impacted on the labour movement in the region in 1921–39. The Special Powers Act (first passed in 1922 and a permanent act from 1933) and the Trade Disputes Act (1927) were both legislated by the inter-war Ulster Unionist Party government of Northern Ireland. Labour activists suffered political discrimination, while they were intimidated through the legislation and their organising was curtailed. Such restrictions effected all those considered 'disloyal' in Northern Ireland. The chapter concludes that in 1921–39 the state of Northern Ireland was administered via a politics of 'disloyalty'; this resulted in a moral economy of loyalty and the peculiar form of the local regime.

Keywords Labour • Law • Loyalty • Moral economy

The state of Northern Ireland was founded in 1921 and consolidated in the inter-war period. Analysts have claimed that this was accomplished through religious discrimination and populist patronage despite the existence of section five of the Government of Ireland Act of 1920. Utilising a case study approach, this chapter examines how two pieces of legislation impacted on the labour movement in the region in the period of 1921 to 1939. The Special Powers Act (first passed in 1922 and a permanent act

© The Author(s) 2018
C. J. V. Loughlin, *Labour and the Politics of Disloyalty in Belfast, 1921–39*, https://doi.org/10.1007/978-3-319-71081-5_4

from 1933) and the Trade Disputes Act (1927) were both legislated by the inter-war Ulster Unionist Party (UUP) government of Northern Ireland. Labour activists suffered political discrimination, while they were intimidated through the legislation and their organising was curtailed. These restrictions were carried out on the basis that the labour movement was considered a 'disloyal' section of the Northern Ireland populace. The chapter concludes that during the period of 1921 to 1939 the state of Northern Ireland state was administered by the UUP through a moral economy of loyalty because of the politicised nature of regional policy. The evidence suggests that as a result of the Government of Ireland Act (1920), all those considered disloyal in Northern Ireland were liable to political discrimination, while those loyal were to be rewarded through patronage.

In the exercise of their power to make laws under this Act neither the Parliament of Southern Ireland nor the Parliament of Northern Ireland shall make a law so as either directly or indirectly to establish or endow any religion, or prohibit or restrict the free exercise thereof, or give a preference, privilege, or advantage, or impose any disability or disadvantage, on account of religious belief or religious or ecclesiastical status.
Legislative Powers, section 5. Prohibition of—laws interfering with religious equality, taking property without compensation, &c.
[10 & 11 George V] Government of Ireland Act, 1920

It all turns on the question of "loyalty" ... the Six Counties is a "loyal" area and it is natural sometimes that "disloyalists" should get hurt ... [and] fail to get jobs. And so on. "Well, they must expect it if they are 'disloyal'," says the outside. But then the outsider does not know that the words "loyalist" and "disloyalist" have a meaning all their own in Northern Ireland.
'Ultach' (pseudonym of James Joseph Campbell), *Orange Terror*, 1943.

A man's religion is entirely his own affair. The point is, there are loyalists and disloyalists.
Viscount Brookeborough, Prime Minister of Northern Ireland, 1943–63, speaking in February, 1969.[1]

In 1979, Patrick Buckland titled his book on the foundation and administration of Northern Ireland in 1921–39 *The Factory of Grievances*. The

---

[1] Quoted in Marc Mulholland, 'Why did Unionists Discriminate?', in *From the United Irishmen to Twentieth-Century Unionism: Essays in Honour of A.T.Q. Stewart* ed. by Sabine Wichert (Dublin: Four Courts Press, 2004), pp. 187–206 (p. 187).

title was based on a quote by the senior Northern Ireland civil servant and former Ulster Volunteer Force and British Army officer, Sir Wilfred Spender. Spender had claimed, whilst writing at the beginning of the Second World War, 'I am afraid there is one other factory we could probably claim that we or the Free State are the largest manufacturers—namely the factory of grievances. I am not at all sure that this particular factory isn't the most paying one in the Province'.[2] Buckland, like Spender, judged the inter-war devolved administration of Northern Ireland unfavourably. In a similar vein to Buckland, the triumvirate of Bew, Gibbon and Patterson—in their important book *Northern Ireland, 1921–72* and subsequent editions—emphasised the role of Protestant working-class pressure in causing the institutionalisation, and elite endorsement, of sectarian practice in the state.[3] Furthermore, in a recent stimulating analysis on gender and religion in twentieth-century Northern Ireland, Brady has claimed that by 1930 'a Protestant state for a Protestant people had been created'.[4] But given the Government of Ireland Act's 'prohibition of laws interfering with religious equality', we are left with a conundrum in the historical evidence: how was a 'Protestant' state constructed if it was explicitly prohibited? This chapter will argue that the inter-war administration of the state in Northern Ireland, perhaps in an attempt to stay within the bounds of section five of the Government of Ireland Act, was a moral economy of loyalty. In this chapter, I utilise the moral economy of loyalty to designate the practice and discourse of regional devolved British state administration in Northern Ireland between 1921 and 1939.[5] The motivation for discriminatory behaviour, however, will not be the main area of consideration in the following chapter.

The moral economy of loyalty clarifies why the regional state, constructed by the UUP, was a *de facto* 'Protestant' state, whilst *de jure* it

[2] Sir Wilfred Spender as quoted in Patrick Buckland, *The Factory of Grievances: Devolved Government in Northern Ireland, 1921–39* (Dublin: Gill and Macmillan, 1979), p. 1.

[3] See Paul Bew, Peter Gibbon, and Henry Patterson, *The State in Northern Ireland, 1921–72: Political Forces and Social Classes* (Manchester: Manchester University Press, 1979); cf. later editions, and, Paul Bew, Peter Gibbon, and Henry Patterson, *Northern Ireland 1921–2001: Political Forces and Social Classes* (revised ed., London: Serif, 2002).

[4] Sean Brady, 'Why Examine Men, Masculinities and Religion in Northern Ireland?', in *Masculinities and Religious Change in Twentieth-Century Britain* ed. by Lucy Delap and Sue Morgan (Basingstoke, 2013), pp. 218–51 (p. 229).

[5] Further research will examine Northern Ireland in 1921–39 anthropologically, culturally, linguistically and historically.

prohibited endorsement of 'any religion'. Charges of malpractice, for example, against the UUP administration of Northern Ireland have been substantiated by balanced enquiry.[6] Other literature substantiated these findings, but there is acceptance that the extent of discrimination was exaggerated and that rhetorical excess was marked amongst ideologues within Ireland and abroad.[7] In contrast to the reconciliatory statements following the foundation of the state in 1921, both UUP politicians and opposition religious figures used extreme rhetoric during the difficult 1930s.[8] Religious and political intolerance was important, as Alvin Jackson has stated, but 'its form and relative significance varied'. He has also pointed to two further 'theoretical constraints' on the administration of Northern Ireland: sovereignty remained in Westminster and section five of the Government of Ireland Act (1920). Jackson is unconvinced by the effectiveness of the section, concluding 'in practice, however, this apparently critical aspect of the constitution does not seem to have been widely invoked'.[9] Arguably, section five of the Government of Ireland Act—and, also, it seems, the experience of the UUP cabinet during the crisis caused by the withholding of Royal Assent to local government electoral reform

---

[6] Cameron Report, Cmnd 532, *Disturbances in Northern Ireland: Report of the Commission appointed by the Governor of Northern Ireland: Presented to Parliament by Command of His Excellency the Governor of Northern Ireland, September 1969* (Belfast: Her Majesty's Stationary Office, 1969); Patrick Buckland, *Factory of Grievances*; Patrick Buckland, *A History of Northern Ireland* (Dublin: Gill & Macmillan, 1981); Patrick Buckland, 'A Protestant State: Unionists in Government, 1921–39', in *Defenders of the Union: A Survey of British and Irish Unionism since 1801* ed. by D. G. Boyce and Alan O'Day (London: Routledge, 2001), pp. 211–26; Marc Mulholland, 'Why did Unionists Discriminate?'; John O'Brien, *Discrimination in Northern Ireland, 1920–39: Myth or Reality?* (Cambridge: Cambridge Scholars, 2010); John Whyte, 'How Much Discrimination was there under the Unionist Regime, 1921–68?' (Manchester: Manchester University Press, 1983) <cain.ulst.ac.uk/issues/discrimination/whyte.htm> [accessed 1 May 2017].

[7] See the discussion amongst sociologists during the 1980s on the extent of discrimination in Northern Ireland. See Conflict Archive on the Internet (CAIN), 'Discrimination-details of source material' <http://cain.ulst.ac.uk/issues/discrimination/soc.htm> [accessed 1 May 2017]; for a dated but still indispensable guide to the above material, consult J. H. Whyte, *Interpreting Northern Ireland* (Oxford: Clarendon Press, 1990).

[8] Compare the infamous statements deployed publicly by UUP politicians in the 1930s, such as Brooke in 1933 and Sir James Craig in 1934, with the historical research presented by Catholic ecclesiastics in the *Down and Connor History Society Journal*. See also Chap. 1, footnote 56.

[9] Alvin Jackson, *Home Rule: An Irish History, 1800–2000* (London: Weidenfeld & Nicolson, 2003), p. 260.

in 1922—circumscribed the extent to which open religious discrimination could be practised by the administration of the state in Northern Ireland.[10] Some commentators, nonetheless, continue to understand the Northern Ireland issue, or problem, as fundamentally about religion.[11] The essentialisation of a religious 'frame' for intra–Northern Ireland relationships can result in the analyst examining the historical record, and society, for 'sectarianism'. But 'sectarianism' was not an 'it' and to proceed in such a manner is to attempt a synchronic analysis of what can only be examined diachronically. Marianne Elliott exemplifies the problem of reifying 'sectarianism': 'Sectarianism operates at many different levels, and people can sustain sectarian systems and pass on sectarianism to their children without ever recognising it in themselves. It is a "distorted expression" of the very basic human needs of belonging and identity. It has also stood in for class struggle in Ireland and usually destroyed any effort at socialist alliance'.[12] In such an analysis, 'it', meaning sectarianism, in this case a Christian-based ethno-religious conflict, is not only sub-conscious *and* conscious but possibly hereditary. Sectarianism also 'stood in for' class conflict and 'usually' destroyed socialist alliance. The adoption of such an essentialised framework of sectarianism involves the danger of mistaking our conceptualisation of the world for the world itself. 'It', confessional division, may have been the motive for politically discriminatory action; but the evidence below suggests that a moral economy of loyalty was the means by which a UUP hegemony was created regionally in Northern Ireland in 1921–39. This framework may account for why the UUP regime co-operated so ineffectively with unions in Northern Ireland[13] and

[10] Single transferable vote proportional representation was introduced for local government elections in Ireland in 1920. In 1922, the Northern Ireland parliament passed a bill to abolish it, the Royal assent was withheld and this precipitated a crisis in Northern Ireland as Craig's government threatened to resign. The crisis was defused only when Royal assent was granted to the bill in December 1922. For extended discussion of Belfast Labour and electoral politics, see Chap. 3.

[11] Steve Bruce, *God Save Ulster: The Religion and Politics of Paisleyism* (Oxford: Oxford University Press, 1989); Steve Bruce, *Paisley: Religion and Politics in Northern Ireland* (Oxford: Oxford University Press, 2007); Sean Brady, 'Men, Masculinities and Religion in Northern Ireland'.

[12] Marianne Elliott, *The Catholics of Ulster: A History* (London: Penguin Books, 2001), p. 5.

[13] Lack of co-operation with unions was relatively unimportant in the quiescent inter-war period. It became a significant problem for industrial relations in the region during the Second World War and after; see Boyd Black, 'A Triumph of Voluntarism? Industrial

why, in a 'Protestant state for a Protestant people', ultra-Protestant dema-
gogues could denounce the UUP as being friendly to Catholicism.[14]

The chapter below will demonstrate that the regional administration of
law and security, in relationship to the labour movement in Northern
Ireland in 1921–39, was on the basis of a political-cultural framework of
'loyalist', 'disloyalist', and associated couplets. Those considered 'disloyal'—primarily, but not confined to, Catholic, republican and labour
activists—suffered victimisation, repression and employment discrimination. This strongly demarcated 'boundary' of loyalty and disloyalty was
constitutive of how the individual, the community, and the law were medi-
ated in the 1920s and 1930s. Furthermore, this framework may have been
an unintended consequence of section five of the Government of Ireland
Act (1920). Section five was intended to prevent religious promotion or
discrimination but in practice politicised the administration of the law and
the state; the section was integral to the political form adopted by the
regional devolved administration. The UUP administration of Northern
Ireland, culturally and politically, constructed a binary discourse of loyalist
and disloyalist: a moral economy of loyalty, an 'old tradition' in a 'new
context'.[15]

The moral economy of loyalty was the 'notion of legitimation' which
facilitated Ulster Unionist administrative hegemony in the Northern
Ireland state in 1921–39. The term 'moral economy' was used by E. P.
Thompson to designate a 'notion of legitimation ... [that men and
women] were informed by the belief that they were defending traditional
rights or customs; and, in general, that they were supported by the wider

Relations and Strikes in Northern Ireland in World War Two', *Labour History Review*, 70
(2005), 5–25; C. J. V. Loughlin, 'Pro-Hitler or Anti-Management? War on the Industrial
Front, Belfast, October 1942', in *Locked Out: A Century of Irish Working-Class Life* ed. by
David Convery (Dublin Academic Press, 2013), pp. 125–39; Emmet O'Connor, *A Labour
History of Ireland, 1824–2000* (second revised ed., Dublin: University College Dublin Press,
2011); Philip Ollerenshaw, 'War, Industrial Mobilisation and Society in Northern Ireland,
1939–1945', *Contemporary European History*, 16 (2007), 169–97.

[14] The UUP government was denounced by Alexander Redpath, a Scottish ultra-Protestant ideologue in the 1930s, as 'a Rome-fearing, priest-puppeting, shilly-shally, namby-
pamby pro-Roman Catholic administration, always on the lookout for doing the Pope a
good turn'. Quoted in Graham Walker, *A History of the Ulster Unionist Party: Protest,
Pragmatism and Pessimism* (Manchester: Manchester University Press, 2004), p. 54.

[15] The phrases 'old tradition' and 'new context' are used by E. P. Thompson, *The Making
of the English Working Class* (re-issued 1980 ed., London: Penguin Classics, 2013), p. 27.

consensus of the community'.[16] He further claimed that 'moral economy' was how 'many "economic" relations are regulated according to non-monetary norms' in peasant and early modern communities.[17] The word 'loyalty' is used by the present author in the sense applied by D. W. Miller in his influential study *Queen's Rebels*. Miller described Victorian and Edwardian Ulster unionism as motivated by 'loyalty', something 'quite different from nationality'. He continued, 'loyalty is a moral principle translated from the realm of personal relationships into politics...it carries the connotations of lawfulness, which Protestants understood to be what distinguished them from Catholic fellow-countrymen'.[18] In particular, the term *moral economy of loyalty* will be used to designate the politico-cultural framework of regional devolved state administration by the UUP in 1921–39.

This chapter will examine two pieces of legislation—the Special Powers Act from 1922 onwards and the 1927 Trade Disputes Act—and the politi-cal reaction of trade unions in one area of partitioned Ireland. The Special Powers Act will be examined first and it will be demonstrated that it was used with political prejudice by the state against those considered disloyal. The second piece of legislation to be examined is the Trade Disputes Act, which was passed in the aftermath of the General Strike in Great Britain in 1926. This act was adopted despite the limited impact the strike had in Northern Ireland. The equivalent British legislation was repealed in 1946, but the equivalent Act was kept on the statue book in a revised form in 1958 in Northern Ireland.[19] The foundation of the state in 1921 gave a distinct framework for the development of a regional political culture. The state and political culture constructed by the ruling administration was maintained by a *moral economy of loyalty*. The chapter will now proceed

[16] E. P. Thompson, 'The Moral Economy of the English Crowd in the Eighteenth Century', in *Customs in Common* (London: Penguin Books, 1993), pp. 185–258 (p. 188).
[17] E. P. Thompson, 'Moral Economy Reviewed', in *Customs in Common* (London: Penguin Books, 1993), pp. 259–351 (pp. 339–40). For a useful introduction to how 'moral econ-omy' has been utilised by historians of eighteenth- and nineteenth-century Ireland, see K.T. Hoppen, *Ireland since 1800: Conflict and Conformity* (2nd ed., London: Longman, 1999), pp. 48–56.
[18] D. W. Miller, *Queen's Rebels: Ulster Loyalism in Historical Perspective* (re-issued 1978 ed., Dublin: University College Dublin Press, 2007), p. 119.
[19] *Hansard Northern Ireland (Commons)*, xliii, 651 (18 Nov. 1958); [7 & 8 Elizabeth II] Trade Disputes and Trade Unions Act, (Northern Ireland) 1958; Tom Boyd, of the NILP, was still querying the existence of provisions from the 1927 Act in January 1969, *Hansard NI (Commons)*, lxxi, 199–200 (21 Jan. 1969).

to the first case study on the Special Powers Act and security policy in Northern Ireland in 1921–39.

4.1 SECTION I: LABOUR AND THE SPECIAL POWERS ACT

Security policy was of supreme importance in the consolidation of the Northern Ireland state in 1921–25: coercive legislation, the Royal Ulster Constabulary (RUC), and auxiliary police units all played a role in securing the new provincial jurisdiction. Although security policy in the new state was shaped by a large number of acts and operations of the state and judicial system, only one act will be analysed and looked at in depth.[20] This is the Civil Authorities (Special Powers) Act (Northern Ireland) of 1922 (the Special Powers Act).[21] The most important piece of security legislation introduced by the Northern Ireland government, the act became notorious for its wide-ranging powers of security, detention, arrest and censorship. Paragraph one of the legislation stated that 'The Civil Authority shall have power … to take all such steps and issue all such orders as may be necessary for preserving the peace and maintaining order'. The 'Civil Authority' referred to the Minister of Home Affairs, his parliamentary secretary or any member of the police to which the minister had delegated his powers.[22] Modelled on the 1914–15 Defence of the Realm Acts and the Restoration of Order in Ireland Act of 1920, the legislation was designed for war and emergency situations.[23] Introduced on an annual basis, it was renewed until 1928, when it was passed for five years. In 1933, it was established permanently. During the inter-war period, the Northern Ireland government's rationale for the Special Powers Act changed from its being deemed necessary to establish stability to its necessity for the maintenance of law and order.[24] The Special Powers Act was authoritarian legislation which could have been granted only as an

[20] For a list of all such acts, see L.K. Donohue, *Counter-Terrorist Law and Emergency Powers in the United Kingdom, 1922–2000* (Dublin: Irish Academic Press, 2007), pp. xx–xxi.

[21] [12 &13 George V] Civil Authorities (Special Powers) Act (Northern Ireland), 1922.

[22] National Council of Civil Liberties (NCCL), *Report of a Commission of Inquiry appointed to examine the Purpose and Effect of the Civil Authorities (Special Powers) Acts of 1922 & 1933* (London, 1936), p. 39.

[23] Colm Campbell, *Emergency Law in Ireland, 1918–25* (Oxford: Clarendon Press, 1994), p. 227; L. K. Donohue, *Counter-Terrorist Law*, p. 17.

[24] L. K. Donohue, *Counter-Terrorist Law*, p. 34.

emergency power, yet it became enshrined permanently in the administration of law and order in 1933. What were the exact provisions of the legislation?

Regulations issued under the Special Powers Act allowed the civil authority to impose curfews, close licensed premises, and prohibit meetings, assemblies or processions. The Civil Authority could close areas, restrict the use of 'motor spirit', direct a member of the security forces to attend a meeting, arrest without warrant, and censor information about the security forces. It could also ban newspapers and prosecute people for the possession or distribution of such material. While the Special Powers Act was arguably necessary for the creation and maintenance of the Northern Ireland state, given the threat posed by Irish Republican Army (IRA) violence in its early years, it curtailed many civil liberties. Freedom of movement, press, association, and *habeas corpus* were all infringed upon. Such legislation, and Unionist arguments in defence of it, encouraged the consolidation of a moral economy of loyalty. All opposition, potential or real, was considered disloyal: the unions and labour movement activists, Catholics, nationalists, republicans, independent unionists, or, even, temperance candidates.

The Special Powers Act, owing to its wide-ranging provisions, also allowed the government to repress the activities of Labour activists, socialists and communists (who were often members and activists in trade unions). The legislation affected unions and their membership as it allowed the state to carry out surveillance of their activities. For example, L. K. Donohue has written, 'the RUC also sent records to the Ministry of Home Affairs regarding various comments made by both MPs and city councillors indicating republican or communist sympathies'.[25] The use of the Special Powers Act for political purposes is in contrast to Unionist insistence that it would not be used in such a manner. Dawson Bates, UUP Minister of Home Affairs, speaking in parliament in 1928, claimed: 'No law abiding citizen in the whole of the north of Ireland is subject today to any harassment by reason of the existence of the [Special Powers] Act. It does not affect the law-abiding citizen; it only operates against the law breakers'.[26] As the National Council of Civil Liberties (NCCL) report of 1936 noted, the Special Powers Act was used by the Northern Ireland government 'towards securing the domination of one particular political

[25] Ibid., 85.
[26] *Hansard NI (Commons)*, ix, 15 May 1928, 1694.

faction and, at the same time, towards curtailing the lawful activities of opponents'.[27] It is clear from the above evidence that the Special Powers Act became normalised into the administration of the province and was deployed against any political opposition to the UUP.

The left continued to utilise parliamentary politics to oppose the Special Powers Act despite the legislative restriction which became a normal operation of the Northern Ireland state. This opposition was often carried out in co-operation with 'disloyal' opposition, such as independent unionists and nationalists. In the parliament of 1925–29, Northern Ireland Labour Party (NILP) MPs opposed the renewal of the Special Powers Act and also proposed amendments to the security budget. In 1926, the NILP MPs voted to halve the amount granted for secret service operations by the RUC[28] and sought to let the Special Powers Act lapse.[29] Nationalist and Labour MPs continued to oppose the estimates for the 'secret service' in the 1930s. The effect that this legislation had on the ability of left-wing activists to organise is demonstrated by the arrest and subsequent court appearances of Belfast communist leader Tommie Geehan in 1934 and 1935. On 11 October 1934, Geehan was arrested under the Special Powers Act for attempting to speak at an Outdoor Relief strike commemoration meeting which had been prohibited.[30] The Belfast Trades Council passed a resolution condemning the Special Powers Act in the wake of Geehan's arrest.[31] Although the Communist Party in Belfast was at this time agitating against the Special Powers Act as part of its united front strategy, opposition was confined to voting resolutions against the Act. In 1936, the NILP conference condemned the Craigavon government's use of the Special Powers Act and called for its repeal.[32] Resolutions were passed against the Special Powers Act by trade unions and left-wing organisations at other times as well.[33]

The control of the person facilitated a confrontational and binary political culture within the region. An example is the surveillance carried

[27] NCCL, *Report of a Commission of Inquiry*, p. 39.

[28] *Hansard NI (Commons)*, vii, 20 April 1926, 583–4.

[29] Ibid., 21 Oct. 1926, 1845.

[30] Inspector General's Office to Ministry of Home Affairs, 16 Oct. 1934 (Public Records Office of Northern Ireland (PRONI), Ministry of Home Affairs files, HA/32/1/550).

[31] Inspector General's Office to Ministry of Home Affairs, 7 Nov. 1934 (PRONI, Ministry of Home Affairs files, HA/32/1/551).

[32] *Belfast Telegraph*, 31 Aug. 1936; *Irish News*, 31 Aug. 1936.

[33] Donohue, *Counter-Terrorist Law*, 113–14.

out by the Northern Ireland government. The vast majority of 'secret' files collated by the Ministry of Home Affairs relate to internment, republicans and nationalists, but there are significant holdings on trade unionists, Labourists, socialists and communists. In the 1920s, the files focus on the NILP, Independent Labour Party (ILP), and trade unions.[34] However, in the 1930s, a shift occurred as the Ministry of Home Affairs identified communists as the major left-wing threat to the state.[35] The Workers' Union was placed under surveillance, and meetings organised by the union and attempts to organise workers were reported on.[36] A strike in Londonderry, a builders' strike, colliery strike and brickworkers' strike were all monitored in case a 'breach of the peace' occurred.[37] There was also a general shipyards' labour disputes file.[38] Surveillance was important for the Ministry of Home Affairs in identifying perceived threats to the power of the Northern Ireland government. One example is provided by International Class War Prisoners Aid (ICWPA), a broad, communist-inspired organisation for prisoners in capitalist countries. Despite being arrested for possession of ICWPA material, Murtagh Morgan was not prosecuted.[39] The Ministry of Home Affairs felt that only if ICWPA grew should police interfere with it. The lack of trade union representatives at an organising meeting was 'noticeable' according to the police.[40] Surveillance was also used to control space and place, facilitating a binary political culture in the region. Exclusion orders,

[34] Co-operation, for example, took place through the activities of the ICWPA in Northern Ireland during the mid-1920s. Emmet O'Connor, *The Reds and the Green: Ireland, Russia, and the Communist Internationals, 1919–43* (Dublin: University College Dublin Press, 2004), p. 110.

[35] Secretary, Ministry of Home Affairs to the Inspector General, RUC, 5 Aug. 1930 (PRONI, Ministry of Home Affairs files, HA/5/1301).

[36] Meetings of the Workers' Union, 1923–24 (PRONI, Ministry of Home Affairs files, HA/5/1307); Meetings of the Workers' Union, 1925–27 (PRONI, Ministry of Home Affairs files, HA/5/1422).

[37] Londonderry City Strike, Building Trade, Ashpit Cleaners, Bacon Curers, Madden Brothers [no date] (PRONI, Ministry of Home Affairs files, HA/5/1352); Strike at Annagher colliery, Coalisland, 1924 (PRONI, Ministry of Home Affairs files, HA/5/1349); Strike, Bricklayers in Belfast, 1923–28 (PRONI, Ministry of Home Affairs files, HA/5/1308).

[38] Labour Disputes in Belfast Shipyards, general file, 1925–30 (PRONI, Ministry of Home Affairs files, HA/5/1448).

[39] E.W. Shewell to Inspector General, RUC, [no date] (PRONI, Ministry of Home Affairs files, HA/32/1/490).

[40] Report of ICWPA in ILP Hall, York Street, Belfast on 6 February 1926 (PRONI, Ministry of Home Affairs files, HA/32/1/490).

which were described as 'unconstitutional' by the NCCL, were used against prominent communists such as Harry Pollitt,[41] Tom Mann[42] and Seán Murray.[43] These men were prominent figures in labour politics, both politically and industrially.

More serious than the general atmosphere of surveillance and repression against trade unions was actual victimisation. James Potts was a civil servant in the British Ministry of Pensions employed in Northern Ireland and he was a member of the ILP.[44] Potts spoke at local labour meetings but was not prosecuted or considered a bad employee by the British government.[45] Yet, by the end of July 1927, Dawson Bates proposed to issue a restriction order on Potts on the grounds that his speeches at ILP meetings might lead to a 'breach of the peace'.[46] Potts was subsequently given one month's notice and dismissed.[47] Potts, as the evidence suggests, was victimised for his political beliefs by his employer, the British Ministry of Pensions. Political interference with other civil servants was also raised by Post Office clerks in 1926 through their trade union.[48]

Further evidence of victimisation is shown with the case of Arthur Griffin. A leading communist in Belfast, Griffin was part of the organising committee for the October 1933 Belfast commemoration of the Outdoor Relief riots of the previous year. The demonstration was prohibited by the government. At a meeting on 24 September 1933, Griffin stated that he wished 'we were able to raise a mass of workers in armed insurrection

---

[41] Kevin Morgan, 'Harry Pollitt', in *Oxford Dictionary of National Biography* online ed. Laurence Goldman <www.oxforddnb.com> [accessed 30 March 2017].

[42] Chris Wrigley, 'Thomas ('Tom') Mann', in Laurence Goldman (online ed.), *Oxford Dictionary of National Biography* online ed. by Laurence Goldman <www.oxforddnb.com> [accessed 30 March 2017].

[43] NCCL, *Report of a Commission of Inquiry*, p. 19; for biographical information on Sean Murray, see Seán Byers, 'Seán Murray's Political Apprenticeship: The Making of an Irish Republican Bolshevik', *Saothar*, 37 (2012), 41–55; Seán Byers, *Seán Murray: Marxist-Leninist and Irish Socialist Republican* (Dublin: Irish Academic Press, 2015).

[44] G. A. Harris to W. Sanger, 4 July 1927 (PRONI, Ministry of Home Affairs files, HA/32/1/516).

[45] W. Sanger to G. A. Harris, 7 July 1927; [R. D. Bates] to James Craig, 11 July 1927 (PRONI, Ministry of Home Affairs files, HA/32/1/516).

[46] R. D. Bates to James Craig, 28 July 1927 (PRONI, Ministry of Home Affairs files, HA/32/1/516).

[47] E. W. Shewell, 24 Aug. 1927 (PRONI, Ministry of Home Affairs files, HA/32/1/516).

[48] *The Gazette: Official Organ of the Northern Ireland Post Office Clerks' Association*, June 1926.

against capitalism'.[49] It was considered by the RUC Inspector General that 'in view of the proposed anniversary of October 11, some action might have a salutary effect on other speakers'.[50] Despite some doubt about the viability of prosecuting Griffin for the above remark,[51] on the transcript of Griffin's speech, dated 4 October, a note states, 'prosecute under the regulations'.[52] At a Cabinet meeting the previous day (3 October), the issue of unemployment was discussed.[53] This evidence suggests the decision to prosecute was agreed on at the Cabinet meeting on 3 October. Griffin claimed his trial was politically motivated, but the Resident Magistrate rejected this claim.[54] Griffin was sentenced to six months in prison. Griffin subsequently died at a sanatorium in Yalta, and local communists claimed his death was partially a consequence of his imprisonment.[55] Victimisation and surveillance were legitimate concerns for the labour movement in inter-war Northern Ireland, but control of public space was similarly contentious.

The prohibition of processions, demonstrations and parades through the Special Powers Act allowed the control of public space by the local administration. Figures given by L. K. Donohue, for example, show that 11 out of 75 banned demonstrations during 1922–39 were Labour-related.[56] Yet one problem with Donohue's categorisation is that Easter commemorations are viewed as being strictly republican.[57] While they were not solely trade union demonstrations, James Connolly's role as a labour organiser in Belfast was a significant aspect of his legacy, especially to members of the NILP, ILP, and later the Socialist Party of Northern

---

[49] Communist meeting, 24 Sept. 1933. Prosecution of Arthur Griffin for Speech Calculated to Lead to a Breach of the Peace (PRONI, Ministry of Home Affairs files, HA/32/1/598).

[50] Inspector General's Office to Ministry of Home Affairs, 27 Sept. 1933 (PRONI, Ministry of Home Affairs files, HA/32/1/598).

[51] Secretary, Ministry of Home Affairs to Inspector General's Office, 30 Sept. 1933 (PRONI, Ministry of Home Affairs files, HA/32/1/598).

[52] Secretary, Ministry of Home Affairs to Inspector General's Office, 3 Oct. 1933 (PRONI, Ministry of Home Affairs files, HA/32/1/598).

[53] Final Cabinet Conclusions, 2 Oct. 1933 (PRONI, Cabinet conclusions, CAB/4/314, 2–3).

[54] *Belfast Newsletter*, 13 Oct. 1933.

[55] *Irish Workers' Voice*, 7 July 1934.

[56] Donohue, *Counter-Terrorist Law*, pp. 74–6.

[57] A problem also demonstrated in B. M. Walker, *A Political History of the Two Irelands: From Partition to Peace* (London: Palgrave Macmillan, 2012), pp. 97–8.

Ireland.[58] The prohibition of demonstrations in Northern Ireland, as is well known, was partially applied. For example, although the Orange Order was initially banned from marching in the summer of 1935, the regional administration rescinded this ban because of the Order's opposition.[59]

The Special Powers Act, an emergency piece of legislation, contributed to the divided political culture of Northern Ireland. The scope and breadth of the Special Powers Act encouraged the construction of a 'zero-sum' mentality between official Unionism and all political opposition in Northern Ireland. Strong executive control was permanently enshrined in statute without provision of proper oversight or equitableness. This resulted in a strongly demarcated boundary of loyalty, politically and culturally. The left was considered disloyal throughout the inter-war period by the UUP administration of the region. As a result, it was condemned to operate as a segment of the disloyal opposition, a situation partially modified by the Second World War. The evidence of the Trade Disputes Act of 1927 in Northern Ireland will now be considered.

4.2   Section II: Labour and the Trade Disputes Act

The post–First World War period witnessed mass industrial struggle across Britain and Ireland. In Ireland these struggles overlapped with disputes over national sovereignty: the Irish Revolution (1917–23).[60] In Britain, industrial struggle centred on the collapse of the post-war boom in 1918–20 which saw cuts in government spending, the lifting of economic controls, and a prolonged level of unemployment. It was also a period of political volatility (for example, the replacement of the Liberal Party by the Labour Party in Britain and the replacement of the Irish Parliamentary Party by Sinn Féin). The general strike of 1926 has been described as the most important industrial struggle of the twentieth century.[61] The strike originated in the mining industry when the owners attempted to cut wages and add an hour to the miners' day. In response, the Miners'

[58] Throughout the period in question, commemorative meetings for James Connolly organised by the left were under surveillance. See, for example, Meetings of North Belfast Socialist Party, 1938 (PRONI, Ministry of Home Affairs files, HA/32/1/562).

[59] Donohue, *Counter-Terrorist Law*, p. 75.

[60] The most authoritative introduction to this contested historiography is Marie Coleman, *The Irish Revolution, 1917–23* (Basingstoke: Routledge, 2013).

[61] Mike Milotte, 'The General Strike and Ireland', in *The Irish Times*, 10 May 1976.

Federation called on transport workers to embargo coal. The most important strike in British industrial history, however, had a modest impact in Northern Ireland. On 4 May, an Emergency Council of unions was formed at a meeting of representatives from 13 trade unions in Northern Ireland which were affiliated with the British Trades Union Congress.[62] An executive of 14 delegates (called the Negotiating Committee) was formed out of the Emergency Council. Yet, despite this preparation, little action relating to the General Strike was taken in Northern Ireland.[63] It was only on 10 May, as the dispute was nearly over, that dockers in Northern Ireland were called out. The Northern Ireland government, by contrast, demonstrated a serious approach to events during 1926.

The Northern Ireland cabinet had prepared for serious industrial trouble locally since August 1925.[64] At that time, there was fear of a railway strike in Ireland, and the Northern Ireland cabinet decided to 'proceed to create, under cover of secrecy, an emergency organisation upon the foundation of the old Supply and Transport Committee'.[65] Preparation was combined with sensitivity to the seriousness of the situation in the country. James Craig, in May 1926, for example, warned that 'provocative' action by the state should be avoided to make sure industrial trouble in Northern Ireland did not escalate.[66] The Northern Ireland government prepared for the General Strike by the passage of an Emergency Powers Act, a 'state of emergency' subsequently being declared by the Governor-General.[67] The Act gave the Northern Ireland government powers similar to those which the British government had assumed through the 1920 Emergency Powers Act. Specifically, the act gave the governor of Northern Ireland power to 'make regulations for securing the essentials of life to the

---

[62] *Belfast Telegraph*, 4 May 1926.

[63] O'Connor, *A Labour History of Ireland, 1824–2000*, p. 196.

[64] Further research on the relationship between industrial and political conflict in Northern Ireland in the twentieth century is necessary. For the background in Derry, see Ronan Gallagher, *Violence and Nationalist Politics in Derry, 1920–3* (Dublin: Four Courts Press, 2003); Emmet O'Connor, *Derry Labour in the Age of Agitation, 1889–1923: 1: New Unionism and Old, 1889–1906* (Dublin: Four Courts Press, 2014).

[65] This committee was formed because of fear of a strike on the railways in both northern and southern Ireland. Final Cabinet Conclusions, 10 Aug. 1925 (PRONI, Cabinet conclusions, CAB/4/147, 3).

[66] Final cabinet conclusions, 3 May 1926 (PRONI, Cabinet Conclusions, CAB/4/167, 1).

[67] [16 & 17 Geo. V] Emergency Powers Act (Northern Ireland), [6 May] 1926; *Belfast Telegraph*, 6 May 1926; *Irish News*, 7 May 1926.

community'. The leadership, however, of the labour movement appears to have settled on a policy of normality. NILP MPs persuaded the Northern Ireland government to include an amendment which prevented regulations to outlaw strikes or picketing.[68] The Northern Ireland government and media, by contrast, appear to have been dynamic in their response. In addition, the lack of a significant challenge in 1926 gave the UUP government confidence to pass the Trades Disputes Act the following year. The Trade Disputes Act of 1927 curtailed many of the legal rights which had previously been won by the trade unions and was a severe blow to the Labour movement across the UK. Though repealed by the Labour Party government in 1946, the equivalent legislation was only amended in Northern Ireland in 1958.[69]

In July 1927, it was agreed with the British Home Office that the Trade Disputes bill in Westminster would be replicated in Northern Ireland, although it was not clear that the Northern Ireland parliament had the power to pass such legislation.[70] When the legislation was debated in the Northern Ireland parliament in the autumn of 1927, Sam Kyle, NILP MP, denounced it as a 'piece of class legislation' and a declaration of 'class war'.[71] He also described it as a 'wicked attack on ... a party that was successful in May last in keeping the peace in this country'.[72] In reply, the Northern Ireland government claimed that the legislation would help the trade unions. J.M. Andrews, UUP Minister of Labour from 1921 to 1937, claimed that passage of the bill was in the interest of trade unionists as it would stop trade union leaders 'embarking on dangerous enterprises'.[73] Lloyd Campbell, UUP MP, stated: 'when a trade union begins to dabble in politics and insists that trade unionists shall subscribe to a political faith they do not believe, then I say they are going outside their proper and legitimate functions'.[74] At stake was the wider power of trade unions, both legally and in society in general.[75] In common with the

---

[68] *Hansard NI (Commons)*, vii, 5 May 1926, 977–82.

[69] See footnote 19 above.

[70] Final Cabinet Conclusions, 13 July 1927 (PRONI, cabinet conclusions, CAB/4/169, 6).

[71] *Hansard NI (Commons)*, viii, 18 Oct. 1927, 2083.

[72] Ibid., 18 Oct. 1927, 2099–100.

[73] *Hansard NI (Commons)*, viii, 19 Oct. 1927, 2180.

[74] Ibid., 19 Oct. 1927, 2154. Campbell's use of the phrase 'political faith' seems to be of some significance.

[75] For an explanation of industrial relations in Northern Ireland, the reader should begin with Boyd Black, 'Reassessing Irish Industrial Relations and Labour History: The

British government, the General Strike was used as an opportunity in Northern Ireland to gain greater legislative power to tackle industrial conflict. This occurred despite the lower level of industrial conflict in Northern Ireland than Britain.[76]

The provisions of the 1927 Trade Disputes and Trade Union s Act (the Trade Disputes Act) altered the rights of trade unions with respect to industrial and political action. First, it made any strike or lockout illegal if it had any objectives other than the furtherance of a trade dispute in which the strikers or employers were engaged.[77] This therefore rendered illegal sympathetic strike action, such as that undertaken by transport and railway workers which had triggered the General Strike. A strike or lockout was deemed illegal if it was 'designed or calculated to coerce the government either directly or by inflicting hardship on the community'. It was similarly illegal to commence, support or give funds to an illegal strike or lockout. Second, no person could be fined, expelled or otherwise punished by their trade union or employer's organisation for refusing to take part in an illegal strike or lockout. This clause led Jack Beattie to describe the Bill as a 'blackleg charter'.[78] Third, it was illegal for one or more people to be at or near a person (or their house, residence, work, business premises or wherever they 'happen to be') to persuade someone to stop work if this was designed to intimidate or would lead to a 'breach of the peace'. Essentially, this provision curtailed the right to picket. Fourth, trade unionists had to 'contract in' to pay the political levy. Fifth, restrictions were placed on the right of civil servants to join trade unions. Sixth, public authorities were not permitted to have a closed shop. Seventh, an injunction could be placed on trade union funds if it was suspected that they would be used in support of an illegal strike. The legislation removed some legal immunity and curtailed democratic rights which had been exercised by trade unions since the nineteenth century.

The restriction of political strike action also represented an important curtailment of trade unions' abilities. NILP MPs remarked that this would have made the 1912 Ulster Covenant illegal as this was, they claimed, a

North-East of Ireland up to 1921', *Historical Studies in Industrial Relations*, 14 (Autumn 2002), 45–97; and O'Connor, *A Labour History of Ireland, 1824–2000*.

[76] K. S. Isles and Norman Cuthbert, *An Economic Survey of Northern Ireland* (Belfast: HMSO, 1957), pp. 232 and 234.

[77] For the exact provisions of the legislation, see [17 & 18 George V] Trade Disputes and Trade Unions Act (Northern Ireland), 1927.

[78] *Hansard NI (Commons)*, viii, 18 Oct. 1927, 2112.

lockout.[79] William McMullen, NILP MP, criticised the 'vagueness' of the legislation.[80] Sam Kyle, NILP MP, stated that a strike in a Comber linen mill could be interpreted as designed to coerce the government because of the ownership of the mill.[81] The bill also removed the indemnity protection provided by the 1906 Trade Disputes Act for illegal strike action.[82] Kyle criticised this clause as one of the most reactionary in the entire Bill.[83] J. M. Andrews, however, rejected the idea that the clause represented a repressive measure; he saw it as only tightening up the laws against illegal strikes.[84] This was factually correct but the wider scope of what could now be designated an 'illegal' strike, and its impact on the ability of rank-and-file trade unionists to take unofficial strike action, meant that it had more significant consequences than the Northern Ireland government wished to publicly admit.

The 1927 Act also financially restricted unions by the introduction of 'contracting in'. The 1913 Trade Union Act had made it legal for trade unions to organise a political fund provided that a vote was taken to set it up and the money was kept in a separate account but this was based upon 'contracting out'. Speaking in Coleraine, Sir M.M. MacNaughten, MP, claimed, a 'good feature of it [the Trade Disputes Bill 1927] was that in future no worker could be compelled to subscribe to the funds of a political party with which he disagreed'.[85] This assertion was countered by NILP MPs who argued that 'contracting out' was easy to do and that trade unions had to vote to establish a political fund before any money could be set aside for political purposes. A stronger argument, from Labour's perspective, was the lack of legal restriction on other political parties' abilities to raise finance.

As parliament prepared to debate the Trade Disputes bill, further pressure was mobilised by the trade unions. A mass meeting chaired by Matthew Courtney of the Amalgamated Engineering Union (AEU), addressed by the British Labour Party MP J. R. Clynes, condemned the bill.[86] An open letter to all MPs from the National Union of Railwaymen

[79] Ibid., 2111.

[80] Ibid., 8 Nov. 1927, 2674.

[81] Many members of the Northern Irish cabinet owned businesses. Kyle's reference alludes to J. M. Andrews's interests in linen and flax. Ibid., 18 Oct. 1927, 2086.

[82] [17 & 18 George V] Trade Disputes and Trade Unions Act (Northern Ireland), 1927.

[83] *Hansard NI (Commons)*, viii, 10 Nov. 1927, 2794.

[84] Ibid., 10 Nov. 1927, 2800.

[85] *Belfast Telegraph*, 1 Oct. 1927.

[86] *Northern Whig*, 20 Sept. 1927.

(NUR) was printed in the press.[87] Pointing out that the bill was designed to 'cripple' the trade unions, both politically and industrially, the NUR called on MPs to oppose it.[88] In the course of the debate, Sam Kyle, MP, pointed to resolutions and letters to MPs from the AEU, Amalgamated Transport & General Workers' Union, and other trade unions protesting at the bill.[89] William Grant, UUP MP, countered that trade unionists in the Ulster Unionist Labour Association (UULA) supported the passage of the bill.[90] Jack Beattie, NILP MP, argued that even the UULA should oppose the bill because if it was passed it would expose that organisation's reactionary outlook to its own members.[91] The bill, as Sam Kyle made clear, was seen as a direct challenge to the Labour movement: 'the government has declared war on organised labour, and I have no doubt that the challenge will be accepted'.[92] The trade unions claimed that they would oppose the bill by every means possible. The Belfast Trades Council attempted to campaign against it, and the NILP planned a campaign against the measure.[93]

The legislation had an impact on both the Outdoor Relief campaign of 1932 and the NUR dispute of 1933. The Outdoor Relief riots of October 1932 occurred after unemployed men struck on 1 October for higher rates of relief from the Poor Law Board in Belfast. As the dispute escalated over the next week and a half, communists agitated for the escalation of the strike. Tommie Geehan, speaking at a mass meeting of 4,000 striking men, stated that 'we have got to try and persuade the organised workers of the city to call a general strike for Tuesday [11 October]'.[94] The Belfast Trades Council and trade union leaders opposed the escalation of the strike,[95] partly as a result the Trade Disputes Act of 1927. A general strike would have been declared illegal and subject to punitive repression.

[87] *Irish News*, 19 Oct. 1927.

[88] Ibid.

[89] *Hansard NI (Commons)*, viii, 18 Oct. 1927, 2083.

[90] Ibid., 19 Oct. 1927, 2129.

[91] Ibid., 2165.

[92] Ibid., 18 Oct. 1927, 2099.

[93] Labour Party (Northern Ireland) Report of Executive Committee to Fifth Annual Conference, 31 Mar. 1928 (PRONI, Records of Sam Napier, 1923–69, D/3702/B/2).

[94] *Irish News*, 6 Oct. 1932.

[95] Mike Milotte, *Communism in Modern Ireland: The Pursuit of the Workers' Republic since 1916* (Dublin: Gill & Macmillan, 1984), p. 129.

The NUR railway dispute of early 1933 was also affected by the legislation. Brian Hanley has described how the IRA co-operated with 'B'
Specials to bomb railway depots, derail locomotives, and snipe at trains.[96]
Railwaymen, who were largely Protestant and loyalist, also accepted help
from communists, the IRA, and Southern workers 'without alarm'.[97]
However, Hanley and Michael Farrell neglect to mention the legislative
context within which the dispute took place. The NUR men had a very
limited range of options to spread the dispute once sympathetic strike
action was ruled out. Similarly, the curtailment of picketing left little room
to escalate the strike. If the repressive legislative context is taken into
account, it is less surprising that trade unionists would have co-operated
with the IRA during this dispute; indeed, Sam Kyle, MP, had warned in
1927 that the legislation would help push trade unionists into 'unconstitutional' action.[98] Between 1921 and 1939, the state in Northern Ireland
set the bounds of legitimate political culture, but the state was administered by the UUP which discriminated in favour of its supporters. The
resulting regional political culture was schismatic and is best described as
a moral economy of loyalty.

4.3   THE MORAL ECONOMY OF LOYALTY, 1921–39

In 1969, as Northern Ireland's democratic *ancien régime* collapsed into
civil strife, John Hewitt penned a biting poem, 'An Ulster Landowner's
Song'.[99] Written at the dusk of landed power in Ulster, it encapsulates the
regional elite's self-perception: proto-aristocratic, country, Orange, and
military. It also summates the 'old tradition' this cultural phenomenon
expressed: the patron-client relationship, between elite and plebeian
Protestant, found in the Orange Lodge and commercialised urban space

[96] Brian Hanley, 'The IRA and Trade Unionism, 1922–72', in *Essays in Irish Labour History: A Festschrift for Elizabeth and John W. Boyle* ed. by Francis Devine, Fintan Lane, and Niámh Puirséil (Dublin: Irish Academic Press, 2008), pp. 157–77 (p. 163).

[97] Michael Farrell, *Northern Ireland: The Orange State* (second ed., London: Pluto Press, 1980), p. 135.

[98] *Hansard NI (Commons)*, viii, 2095 (18 Oct. 1927).

[99] John Hewitt, first appeared in *Tribune*, 2 Sept. 1969; re-printed in John Hewitt, *An Ulster Reckoning* (Coventry: Privately published, 1971); see also W. J. McCormack, *Northman: Joh Hewitt, 1907–87: An Irish Writer, His World, and His Times* (Oxford: Oxford University Press, 2015), pp. 201–2.

of early modern Ulster.[100] The 'populists' of the UUP, for example, were imperial, aristocratic, Orangemen, and politicians; they were not administrators.[101] They organised the 'sports', met their tenants, and attended Church, the Lodge, and Market. The poem contextualises the 'frame' adopted by Unionist intellectuals in the inter-war period; this was a perspective and politics which concentrated on the seventeenth-century plantation roots of Ulster.[102] For Cyrill Falls, historian and British Army officer in the Ulster Volunteer Force, the plantations in the early 1600s in Ulster were literally and metaphorically *The Birth of Ulster*. Given the early modern origin of the region's Protestant community, the nineteenth-century roots of political Ulster Unionism, and the twentieth-century creation of Northern Ireland, the moral economy of loyalty was the 'old tradition' by which a regional Unionist hegemony was created in a 'new context' in 1921–39. The moral economy of loyalty—in 1920s and 1930s Northern Ireland—involved early modern cultural forms in the administration of regional governance.

This chapter examined how two pieces of legislation constituted major grievances to labour in the region and how both were applied with political partiality. The Special Powers Act normalised emergency security legislation into day-to-day governance and contributed to the 'siege mentality' maintained by the UUP in Northern Ireland. The Trade Disputes Act 1927, through its criminalisation of activities previously legal, resulted in co-operation between groups who made uneasy bedfellows, such as during the NUR strike. This act was, perhaps, passed with an understanding that it could contribute to dealing with consumer boycotts, strikes and lockouts. Both pieces of legislation, however, point to the 'zero-sum' mentality fostered by the UUP's administration of the region in 1921–39. This understanding of how the local elite envisioned governance may also

---

[100] The cultural, spatial and temporal connections between Ulster and the early modern British state—through the Covenant in the seventeenth and twentieth centuries, for example—make 'moral economy' a term worthy of further use while researching the history of the Northern Ireland state.

[101] 'Populist' is how Bew *et al.* described the clique of the UUP associated with Craig, J. M. Andrews; 'anti-populist' was used to describe the clique, associated with Spender, who were less inclined to utilise the state for explicit patronage reasons. See Bew, Gibbon, and Patterson, *Northern Ireland 1921–2001*.

[102] Cyrill Falls, *The Birth of Ulster* (London: Methuen, 1936); Cyrill Falls, *Elizabeth's Irish Wars* (London: Methuen, 1950); Gillian McIntosh, *The Force of Culture: Unionist Identities in Twentieth-Century Ireland* (Cork: Cork University Press, 1999), pp. 25–7.

account for the relatively poor industrial relations record of employers during the UUP administration of the Northern Ireland state. The evidence for the implementation of both pieces of legislation in relationship to labour indicates a moral economy of loyalty in the devolved, highly politicised, regional administration of the British state.

The moral economy of loyalty was the 'moral principle' and 'personal relationship in politics' by which all opposition to the UUP was construed as disloyalty to the state.[103] Spender and Buckland's 'factory of grievances' remains a stunningly evocative metaphor for the political culture of the region. But the moral economy of loyalty accounts for the form of the Northern Ireland state, a *de facto* 'Protestant' state, whilst *de jure* it prohibited endorsement of 'any religion'. The form of a moral economy facilitated political discrimination against opponents, for whatever reason, whilst insincerely maintaining section five of the Government of Ireland Act (1920). This discourse enabled political discrimination against not only the labour movement but all those considered disloyal by the ruling administration in Northern Ireland in 1921–39.

---

[103] D. W. Miller, *Queen's Rebels*, p. 119.

CHAPTER 5

Women and Belfast Labour Politics

Abstract Women's history has become an important area of historiography in Ireland since the 1970s, but gender is still under-researched. This chapter first examines the social, economic and political position of women locally and how Belfast labour constructed understandings of sexual division and the 'masculine' and the 'feminine'. The chapter also examines the recent analysis of gender in Northern Ireland by Sean Brady and Jane G.V. McGaughey and their use of 'hegemonic masculinity'. It concludes that the local labour movement was dominated by assumptions related to masculinity and a prioritisation of men's issues. This was displayed, for example, in the demand for a 'family wage' and the confinement, in the main, of trade unionism to men.

Keywords Belfast • Women • Gender • Labour • Loyalty

5.1 'On Whom Will She Smile?'

Illustration 5.1 is indicative of the increasing importance of feminine political agency during the inter-war period. The 1918 Representation of the People Act enfranchised women over 30 years of age, but there remained the issue of enfranchisement of younger women, or the so-called

© The Author(s) 2018
C. J. V. Loughlin, *Labour and the Politics of Disloyalty in Belfast,
1921–39*, https://doi.org/10.1007/978-3-319-71081-5_5

'flapper' vote.[1] If we examine the foreground of the illustration, the 'Queen' exemplifies the modern young woman of the late 1920s: stylish, wearing the latest fashion, a slim waist as opposed to the late Victorian and Edwardian fashion for the accentuation of female hips. Of more significance for the present book, however, are the background and the question addressed to the young woman: 'On Whom Will She Smile?' The last case study in this book examines the social and economic position of women in Belfast in 1921–39. It also addresses female political agency and its relationship to the politics of masculinity.

The 'Queen of the May' is a clear representation of the binary political culture established in inter-war Belfast and Northern Ireland. It portrays a binary opposition between Unionist (a union flag can be seen in the uppermost left corner) and 'Opposition' and 'Opposition Party'. It is an explicit representation of the politics of Northern Ireland in 1921–39: a 'zero-sum' game centred on loyalist and disloyalist, a moral economy of loyalty. Also, the control and dominance exerted by the Ulster Unionist administration of Northern Ireland were often politics as a policing action.[2] This moral economy of loyalty was the means by which the Ulster Unionist Party (UUP) of Northern Ireland discriminated against those considered disloyal, both Irish Nationalists and Labour. The development of women's history and, more recently, gender history are entwined (Fig. 5.1).

In the 1970s, women's history began to develop significantly in Ireland, yet gender history is still a relatively under-researched phenomena on the island.[3] There has, however, recently developed stimulating analysis of masculinities and gender in Northern Ireland during the twentieth century. J.G.V. McGaughey, for example, has detailed the construction of a Protestant Unionist masculinity as the hegemonic masculinity in the

---

[1] In 1927–28, there was a campaign in Britain against the so-called 'flapper vote'. See Adrian Bingham, *Gender, Modernity and the Popular Press in Inter-War Britain* (Oxford: Clarendon Press, 2004), p. 113 (pp. 135–9).

[2] Jacques Rancière, *Disagreement: Politics and Philosophy* (Minnesota: University of Minnesota Press, 2004), p. xiii.

[3] Maria Luddy, 'Gender and Irish History', in *The Oxford Handbook of Modern Irish History* ed. by Alvin Jackson (Oxford: Oxford University Press, 2014), pp. 193–213; see also Mary McAuliffe, 'Irish Histories: Gender, Women and Sexualities', in *Palgrave Advances in Irish History* ed. by Mary McAuliffe, Katherine O'Donnell and Leeann Lane (Basingstoke and New York: Palgrave Macmillan, 2009), pp. 191–221.

Fig. 5.1 'The "Queen of the May" 1929. On Whom Will She Smile?'. Source: *Belfast Telegraph*, 11 May 1929

region.[4] Similarly, Brady has analysed the issue of 'hegemonic masculinities' in relationship to Northern Ireland.[5] However, problems with such analyses are the use and definition of the term 'hegemony' and related issues of gender construction and occupational divisions. This chapter will therefore seek to investigate 'hegemonic masculinities' in Belfast in 1921–39. This case study will present some evidence which qualifies the extent of hegemonic masculinity in inter-war Belfast. It will do this by examining, first, the social, economic and cultural position of women in Belfast in the first half of the twentieth century. Second, it will examine women's politics in Belfast as represented by Labour, Ulster Unionism and Irish Nationalism. Last, the chapter will turn to McGuaghey and Brady's analyses to see how they compare with the evidence presented above. So what was the position of women in early twentieth-century Belfast?

[4] J. G. V. McGaughey, *Ulster's Men: Protestant Unionist Masculinities and Militarization in the North of Ireland, 1912–1923* (Montréal: McGill-Queen's University Press, 2012).
[5] Sean Brady, 'Why Examine Men, Masculinities and Religion in Northern Ireland?', in *Masculinities and Religious Change in Twentieth-Century Britain* ed. by Lucy Delap and Sue Morgan (Basingstoke, 2013), pp. 218–51.

5.2   To 'Make Men of You All'

Both left-wing and feminist politics developed in Belfast in the 1890s; this is related to the developments of 'new unionism' and feminism across Britain and Ireland in this decade. In Belfast, this was demonstrated, for example, when the Women's Trade Union League helped to found three new unions for textile workers in the city in the early 1890s. The Textile Operatives' Society of Ireland (TOSI) was founded in 1893, and Mary Galway became secretary in 1897.[6] Mary Galway was an important Irish woman trade unionist before the First World War; she played a key role in the development of female trade unionism in Ireland and its relationship to the state. Galway was a member of the delegation which met the Liberal Chief Secretary for Ireland, Augustine Birrell, in 1907. Female delegates were also beginning to play a role at the Irish Trades Union Congress, although female delegates remained in single figures up to the First World War.[7] These radical and reformist efforts represented the first tentative steps towards female trade unionism in Ireland.

Low pay, casualisation, long hours and poor conditions were common experiences for working women in Belfast prior to 1914. Conditions in the textile industry, for example, were delineated by Mary Galway, one of the pioneers of female trade unionism in the north, in a reminiscence entitled, 'Conditions in the Linen Industry in the North'.[8] Galway described how 'in Ulster linen permeates every phase of life'.[9] From a capitalisation of £2.5 million in 1853, the industry in the north had progressed to £50 million. Low pay and bad conditions meant that many textile workers were forced to emigrate, a situation only slightly altered by the better wages of the First World War in the industry. Furthermore, Galway described the division of labour via sex in Belfast occupations:

---

[6] Mary Galway, 'The Linen Industry in the North of Ireland: And the Betterment of Working Conditions', in *The Voice of Ireland: A Survey of the Race and Nation from All Angles* ed. by W. G. Fitzgerald (Dublin and London: Virtue and Company Limited, 1924), pp. 295–8; also re-produced in the *Field Day Anthology of Irish Writing* ed. by Angela Bourke *et al.*, 5 vols. (Cork: Cork University Press, 2002), *V: Irish Women's Traditions and Writings*, pp. 555–7.

[7] See M. E. Daly, 'Women and Trade Unions' (pp. 106–16) and 'Women and the Trade Union Movement' (pp. 357–70), in *Trade Union Century* ed. by Donal Nevin (Cork: Mercier Press, 1994).

[8] Mary Galway, 'The Linen Industry in the North of Ireland', p. 295.

[9] Ibid.

Belfast has in normal times plenty of work for both sexes; in the shipyards and engineering establishments for men and in the mills, factories and warerooms for women…Three females are employed for one male. You will find whole families of girls in the mills or factories—sometimes the mother and several daughters. The spinners and weavers of today are the daughters and grand-daughters of spinners and weavers, so that skill runs in the blood; there are today in no part of the world more competent textile workers than the women of Ulster.[10]

Galway, however, also explicated two other areas of note: the necessity of a family income and the role of 'home work'. The low pay and economic structure in the north of Ireland necessitated that:

the wife and mother had to go back to the mill or factory as well as her husband, as it required the combined earnings to make both ends meet at home. The effects of this system-which still prevails-need not be enlarged upon; it was, and is, bad for the state, bad for the community and the family.[11]

Last, Galway described the conditions of those textile workers involved in 'home work'. The Belfast Medical Officer of Health, Dr. H. W. Baillie, drew attention to these workers in 1910. These women workers took work home and finished it, re-delivering it to the employer the next day. This was difficult and 'sweated' work: for example, one worker, at the rate of 1d per cushion and 300 dots per cushion, earnt just 6d a day. These workers, according to Baillie, were 'grossly underpaid, and their health was adversely affected'.[12] In 1915, these workers would be included in the textile Trade Board set-up, although trade boards played a relatively minor role in inter-war industrial relations.[13] Galway's description is invaluable for illustrating the difficult conditions facing women at work and female trade unionism. The conditions described above, by Galway, form the context for the next wave of female trade unionism in Ireland: the development of trade unionism associated with Larkin, Connolly and the Irish Transport and General Workers' Union (ITGWU).

[10] Mary Galway, 'The Linen Industry in the North of Ireland', p. 296.
[11] Ibid., p. 297.
[12] Ibid., pp. 297–8.
[13] The most detailed investigation of this topic is B. M. Brown, 'Trade Boards in Northern Ireland, 1909–45' (unpublished PhD thesis, Queen's University Belfast, 1999).

The Irish Women Workers' Union (IWWU) was set-up as an all-female trade union in September 1911 by female trade union activists and other radicals.[14] The IWWU was formed as a complement to the ITGWU. Masculine assumptions about trade unionism and citizenship seem to have played a part in the foundation of the IWWU. For example, Countess Markievicz stated at the IWWU's founding meeting:

> Without organisation you can do nothing and the purpose of this meeting is to form you into an army of fighters...As you are all aware women have at present no vote, but a union such as has now been formed will not alone help you obtain better wages, but will also be a means of helping you to get votes...and thus make men of you all.[15]

Jim Larkin also stated that 'women are the basis of a nation's wealth. On them practically depends the efficiency and welfare of the race. Good or bad, the men are what the women made them'.[16] The role of politics, economics, culture and gender intersected with female trade unionism. However, Mary Galway and the TOSI, addressing the Belfast Trades Council in 1911, claimed that the IWWU was poaching members from their union. Underlying this inter-union rivalry was the inability of Galway or the TSOI to organise the less well-paid workers in the linen industry. These workers tended to be Protestant and this further implies that IWWU and TOSI competition may have been driven by confessional division, skill division, pay and inter-union rivalry. By 1914, however, female trade unionism had definitively developed in Ireland. Women's ability to organise separately and to sustain female trade unionism had been demonstrated. Women were also playing a role in the feminist, Ulster Unionist and Irish Nationalist movements in Ireland, whilst the Irish Citizens' Army took the radical step of allowing women to serve in frontline positions alongside men.

The trade unionism that developed, nevertheless, remained the preserve of better-paid sections of the workforce. Skill, generational and communal division may all have contributed to the above-mentioned competition between Mary Galway's TOSI and the ITGWU-associated IWWU. In common with women's trade unionism, trade unions for the

[14] Mary Jones, *These Obstreperous Lassies: A History of the Irish Women Workers' Union* (Dublin: Gill & Macmillan, 1988), p. 1.
[15] Ibid.
[16] Ibid., p. 2.

unskilled became a serious and organised force only with the development of 'new unionism'.[17] The textile industry granted a distinctive employment profile for Belfast and the north of Ireland: for example, in 1926, 21% of married women in the north were employed, a figure four times greater than the rate in southern Ireland.[18] Alongside skill divisions in the labour force then, there were generational, sexual, religious and political divisions. Generational divisions were a product of the kinship relations encouraged in the workplace, whilst certain trades, and jobs and occupations within trades, were reserved for either sex. Furthermore, religious division correlated with wealth disparities between the communities in Belfast, Ireland and Britain. The better-paid jobs tended to be the preserve of the better educated, skilled and wealthier, all of which favoured the Protestant communities over the Catholic. These cultural, social and economic divisions were given explicit political and cultural form in the 1900s by Unionist, Nationalist and Labour politics.

5.3   War, Women and Economics

The First World War had a significant impact upon Ireland, although its effects were attenuated by comparison with Britain.[19] For example, women were utilised in significant numbers for auxiliary roles such as nursing. This was combined with voluntary war work for those from the elite and middle class. The war itself both changed and rejuvenated the division of public life via sexual division: single men in Britain, for example, were conscripted from early 1916, whilst married men were called up later that year; women, in contradistinction, were drafted into auxiliary positions and also utilised in traditionally male-only occupations on the 'home front'. The acute need for labour in Britain widened women's employment during wartime. In the first six months of the war, large numbers of

[17] See Emmet O'Connor, *Syndicalism in Ireland, 1917–23* (Cork: Cork University Press, 1988); and Conor Kostick, *Revolution in Ireland: Popular Militancy, 1917–23* (second ed., Cork: Cork University Press, 2009), pp. 13–18 (pp. 192–213).

[18] Myrtle Hill, *Women in Ireland: A Century of Change* (Belfast: Blackstaff Press, 2003), pp. 99–100.

[19] D. Fitzpatrick, 'Militarism in Ireland, 1900–22', in *A Military History of Ireland* ed. by Thomas Bartlett and Keith Jeffery (Cambridge: Cambridge University Press, 1996), pp. 379–406; Keith Jeffery, *Ireland and the Great War* (Cambridge: Cambridge University Press, 2000); *Ireland and the Great War: A War to Unite Us All?* ed. by Adrian Gregory and Senia Paseta (Manchester: Manchester University Press, 2002).

skilled men volunteered to fight and endangered the viability of production. One solution was to 'comb out' such skilled labour from enlistment, whilst another was the Treasury Agreement of March 1915. This agreement relaxed trade union and craft practice in the workplace. The traditional sexual division of occupations was undermined with the implementation of 'dilution' in the workplace. Dilution allowed unskilled and semi-skilled labour to be utilised for previously controlled, skilled occupations. For example, most craft apprenticeships lasted seven years, whilst dilution allowed a worker to be trained within six months. These developments of war and work affected Ireland and Britain differently. The demand for female labour, owing to the lack of conscription, was never as great in Ireland as in Britain. Yet the first section of Britain's home front to collapse was Ireland in Easter 1916.[20]

Women played an explicit role in the separatist Easter Rebellion of 1916 and subverted gender expectations of the period. The role of Constance Markievicz, for example, is well known and explicitly subverted dominant gender assumptions in both Britain and Ireland. But, recently, further attention has been given to other female participants. Helena Moloney, who re-organised the IWWU alongside Connolly in 1915, took part in the Easter Rising and was interned until December 1916. Winnifred Carney, Connolly's aide-de-camp, similarly subverted gendered norms. Overall, according to Fearghal McGarry, approximately 200 women took part in the Easter Rising in a number of different organisations.[21] Women were largely confined to auxiliary positions, but the fighting in Dublin during Easter Week meant that auxiliary support was essentially a frontline role. The subversive militarised role played by women was not highlighted, however, in the immediate aftermath or the popular memory of 1916. The public and popular memory of 1916 highlighted the traditional, masculinised nature of the violence. Women were utilised politically as widows or kin relations to dead separatists as part of this process. This symbolic role was effective politically but was at the expense of downgrading the contribution made by women during Easter Week 1916.

Politically, women in the UK were rewarded for their role in the war effort by the enfranchisement of women over 30 in the Representation of the People Act (1918). This Act radically shifted the social bases of

---

[20] See Marie Coleman, *The Irish Revolution, 1917–23* (Basingstoke: Routledge, 2013) and Fearghal McGarry, *The Rising: Easter 1916* (Oxford: Oxford University Press, 2010).

[21] Fearghal McGarry, *The Rising*, p. 161.

electoral politics in both Ireland and Great Britain.[22] For example, the electorate approximately trebled between the 1910 and 1918 elections. In Ireland, the electorate was 700,000 in 1910 but was 2 million in 1918. In Belfast, the electorate expanded from 80,500 to 172,000 during the same years.[23] In the UK, the post-war period saw the decline of the Liberals as a governing party, whilst in Ireland Sinn Féin replaced the Irish Parliamentary Party (IPP) as the major electoral force. It was only in Ulster that the IPP managed to retain some five seats, although this was a result of a pact between republican separatists and nationalists in the province.

However, the First World War and after were contradictory in their effects on women. There were increased employment opportunities and partial enfranchisement of women, but the pre-war occupational sexual division of labour was re-established. For example, women were forced out of new areas of employment in munitions work by a 1919 act: The Restoration of Pre-War Practices Act. The 1919 Restoration Act was the *quid pro quo* of the 1915 Treasury Agreement: trade union and craft practices were relaxed in munitions production, but with the tacit understanding this was only for the duration of the First World War. However, in 1918, it was still unclear that trade practice and customs would be reinstated after the war. Despite this lack of clarity, N. C. Soldon has commented that '[in 1918 and 1919] employers were quick to co-operate with skilled workers in expelling women from their jobs so that production during the post-war boom was not interrupted'.[24] The re-imposition of marriage bars, whereby a woman had to resign from her employment on her marriage, formed another aspect of the counter-revolutions which women faced during the inter-war period.[25] Other areas of employment, which had expanded to include women during wartime, now contracted for women. There are many aspects to the question of female employment in the period—technological change and the overall demand and supply of labour in the British and Irish economies, for example—but the most politically charged in 1919 was the ex-Servicemen issue. The UK post-1918 was faced with the daunting task of re-employing 5 million ex-Servicemen into the peacetime economy.

[22] There is a voluminous literature on this issue in both Britain and Ireland.
[23] A. C. Hepburn, *Catholic Belfast and Nationalist Ireland in the Era of Joe Devlin, 1871–1934* (Oxford: Oxford University Press, 2008), pp. 198 and 200.
[24] N. C. Soldon, *Women and Trade Unions, 1874–1976* (Dublin: Gill & Macmillan, 1978), p. 100.
[25] See Myrtle Hill, *Women in Ireland*; and R. C. Owens, *A Social History of Women in Ireland, 1870–1970* (Dublin: Gill & Macmillan, 2005).

Ireland was affected by these issues too, although the lack of conscription meant that its experience of wartime manpower was less acute than that experienced in Britain. Furthermore, this post-war dislocation and resentment correlate with the workplace expulsions in east Ulster in the summer of 1920.[26]

5.4   Women and the Politics of Labour in Belfast, 1921–39

The social conditions which women faced in Belfast in the inter-war period were difficult. Infant mortality, for example, was worse than in many comparable British cities; this occurred even though Belfast had a lower infant mortality rate than the aforementioned British cities in 1900.[27] Munck and Rolston have pointed out that 'other cities had improved their care of young mothers and young children at a much faster rate than Belfast in the first third of the century'.[28] Belfast also had higher rates of mortality for a number of infectious diseases, such as tuberculosis, than the English average.[29] The combination of poor infant and maternal mortality, poverty, high unemployment and comparatively high rates of infectious disease meant that social conditions were harsh for working-class women in Belfast in 1921–39. However, the population of the city did continue to rise during the period and housing conditions marginally improved.[30]

As a specific economic group, women were worse off than men. Of those gainfully occupied in Northern Ireland, according to the 1926 census, only 31.6% were women.[31] Wages were also often inferior as women were 'generally employed at lower rates than men'.[32] The minimum wage rates paid to women working in 14 light industries were approximately 57% of the wage rate paid to men (in both 1925 and 1936).[33] Despite the prominent role they had played in war industries during the First World

[26] See Chap. 2.
[27] Ronnie Munck and Bill Rolston, *Belfast in the Thirties: An Oral History* (Belfast: Blackstaff Press, 1987), p. 74.
[28] Ibid.
[29] Ibid., pp. 72–3.
[30] See Chap. 3 above.
[31] *Ulster Year Book 1929* (Belfast: HMSO, 1929), p. 19.
[32] K. S. Isles and Norman Cuthbert, *An Economic Survey of Northern Ireland* (Belfast: HMSO, 1957), p. 285.
[33] Isles and Cuthbert, *Economic Survey of Northern Ireland*, p. 226.

War, women were expected to leave employment when they married.[34] Marriage bars were re-introduced during the inter-war period, forcing women to leave work, in certain occupations, once married. Women's employment was predominantly in sectors which, with the benefit of hindsight, were in long-term economic decline. For example, women made up 42.8% of those employed in manufacturing (owing to their role in textile production) and 73.1% in personal service.[35] Table 5.1 illustrates that women represented approximately half of all trade unionists in Northern Irish–based unions. By contrast, women

Table 5.1 Gender composition of Northern Irish and British-based trade union membership in Northern Ireland, 1922–36

Year	Northern Irish-based trade unions			British-based trade unions		
	Total	Male	Female	Total	Male	Female
1921	24,511	9634	14,877	n/a	n/a	n/a
1922	16,957	6969	9988	n/a	n/a	n/a
1923	15,438	7041	8397	n/a	n/a	n/a
1924	14,833	7198	7635	n/a	n/a	n/a
1925	14,575	6450	8125	n/a	n/a	n/a
1926	12,413	5157	7256	n/a	n/a	n/a
1927	10,334	4469	5865	55,107	51,135	3972
1928	8938	3850	5088	53,063	49,941	3122
1929	8885	3867	5018	54,844	52,188	2656
1930	8656	3951	4705	56,272	53,274	2548
1931	8084	3645	4439	60,321	57,789	2532
1932	7480	3306	4174	54,024	51,876	2148
1933	7580	3545	4035	49,769	47,636	2133
1934	8808	4293	4515	55,200	53,070	2130
1935	8904	4451	4453	62,556	56,607	5949
1936	9293	4599	4694	66,052	59,374	6678

Source: *Ulster Year Book 1926*, p. 112; *Ulster Year Book 1929*, pp. 109–10; *Ulster Year Book 1932*, pp. 128–9; *Ulster Year Book 1935*, p. 138; *Ulster Year Book 1938*, p. 163

Note: Separate returns for the Northern Ireland membership of British-based unions are unavailable, 1921–26, *Ulster Year Book 1926*, p. 111; the [17 & 18 George V] Trade Disputes and Trade Unions Act (Northern Ireland), 1927, meant that these unions had to furnish membership statistics to the local administration; see *Ulster Year Book 1929*, p. 109

[34] Munck and Rolston, *Belfast in the Thirties*, p. 119.

[35] *Ulster Year Book 1929*, p. 19; see also the work of Myrtle Hill and R. C. Owens, noted above, for discussion of women's employment in Ireland, north and south, in the twentieth century.

constituted only a small minority of the membership of British-based trade unions. As can be seen, women represented only a minority of local trade union membership in Northern Ireland. Female trade unionism was, however, now established as a viable section of the labour movement. Comparatively, however, Northern Ireland had a low trade union density of the insured female workforce: 7% as opposed to a corresponding figure of 21% in Britain.[36] Given the level of employment of women in Northern Ireland—31.6% were gainfully occupied in 1926—they were significantly under-represented in the labour movement. The tough economic conditions of the inter-war period, the continued predominance of craft and skilled trade unions, and the return to pre-war trade practice resulted in women's under-representation within trade unionism. In the 1930s, labour activists adopted a strategy of 'wait and see'.[37] These conditions began to change at the end of the 1930s.[38] What policies, however, were adopted by the Belfast labour movement to appeal to women?

The Northern Ireland Labour Party (NILP) appealed to women with certain policies. Policies on education and welfare were broadly, though not exclusively, designed to appeal to women. The NILP's key policy on education was the provision of free education from primary to third level.[39] The theme of free education appears continually in NILP electoral statements throughout the inter-war period. Labour politicians also espoused the cause of free schoolbooks for children. Despite some UUP opposition to the policy (on the basis that it would make children dependent on charity),[40] there were members of the UUP who also advocated it. Alderman Duff, of the UUP, for example, stated in 1929 that a policy of free schoolbooks would be implemented but only if it did not involve putting the rates up. This suggests that it was a popular policy. The Central Women's Section of the NILP canvassed Dock ward with petitions in support of free schoolbooks, indicating that the NILP actively campaigned on the issue. However, the policy of free education does not appear to have

---

[36] Emmet O'Connor, *A Labour History of Ireland, 1824–2000* (second revised ed., Dublin, 2011), p. 194.

[37] David Bleakley, *Saidie Patterson: Irish Peacemaker* (Belfast: Blackstaff Press, 1980), p. 17.

[38] Ibid., pp. 26–7.

[39] *Irish News*, 8 Jan. 1924.

[40] *Belfast Newsletter*, 11 Jan. 1929.

been fully thought out in practical terms and was perhaps a reflection of British Labour Party influences.

An important welfare policy propagated by the NILP was the extension of health services, especially those which related to maternal and child welfare. Members of the party linked poor social conditions in Belfast to the UUP administration and Northern Ireland government. For example, Hugh Gemmell attributed the high infant mortality rate to 'the bad housing and other conditions perpetuated by the Unionists in the Corporation'.[41] Similarly, Sam Kyle, NILP MP, claimed that the UUP was too busy looking at other issues to 'look at one of the most important': maternal and child welfare.[42] Ida Boyd, an NILP Corporation candidate in 1930, called for the Belfast Corporation to change its attitude of keeping the rates as low as possible and instead become 'anxious to save babies rather than the rates'.[43] Mary Kyle also criticised the Corporation as 'always counting the cost' of maternal and child welfare rather than being anxious to save lives.[44]

In 1924, the NILP also founded a Central Women's Section. The Central Women's Section prompted numerous motions on the issue of maternal welfare to be adopted by the party.[45] Members of the section were co-opted onto the Belfast Corporation Maternal and Child Welfare Committee and also lobbied Dawson Bates a number of times on the issue.[46] How much of an impact the section had is not clear, but many of the policies espoused by the NILP were adopted in the post–Second World War period. For example, the party called for a state Ministry of Health in Northern Ireland. Similarly, the NILP advocated family allowances, replicating the British Labour Party position, and this policy was introduced during the Second World War and continues, in a modified form, up to the present. Therefore, conditions for women economically, politically and socially were difficult, but the labour movement had a number of means to appeal to women. The next section will examine women and politics in Belfast during the inter-war period.

[41] *Irish News*, 12 Jan. 1928.
[42] *Northern Whig*, 8 Jan. 1929.
[43] Ibid., 10 Jan. 1930.
[44] Ibid.
[45] Minute book of the Central Women's Section of the Northern Ireland Labour Party, 1924–32 (Public Records Office of Northern Ireland, PRONI, D/3311/1).
[46] Ibid.

5.5   Women's Politics in Belfast, 1921–39

Women played an important organisational role in Irish politics in the first half of the twentieth century, but Diane Urquhart has claimed that this is apparent only when a 'high political' perspective is transcended.[47] The preceding analysis seconds Urquhart's argument. Women, for example, continued to play a significant role in the auxiliary organisations of Irish nationalism and Ulster Unionism. In 1919, there were 23 auxiliary female lodges of the Orange Order and 10 women's auxiliary branches of the Ancient Order of Hibernians.[48] Similarly, the Ulster Women's Unionist Council (UWUC) provided a forum for women to be involved politically.[49] In the 1925 Northern Ireland general election, Urquhart has explained, 'women were very pro-active-canvassing, providing assistance in tally rooms and escorting electors to the polls'.[50] However, the auxiliary and subordinate role women played in politics is demonstrated by the lack of women elected in inter-war Northern Ireland. Between 1921 and 1940, for example, there were only three women UUP MPs and no Labour or Nationalist women MPs.[51] The Ulster Unionist Labour Association (UULA) refused to allow women members, on the grounds that there were already political organisations in existence for women.[52] In municipal politics in Belfast, there were few women elected to the corporation. The position, however, was slightly better on the Board of Guardians where women had a longer record of participation. In the years 1921–40, there were a minimum of seven and a maximum of 10 women Guardians in Belfast.[53]

The UWUC was formed on the 23 January 1911 and it is estimated that, by 1912, upto 120,000 women had joined the organisation, conceivably making it the largest female political organisation in Ireland at the time. The UWUC played a central role in mobilising women for Ulster Day, 28 September 1912. They mobilised women to sign a complementary women's declaration alongside the men's Covenant. Unionist women,

[47] Diane Urquhart, *Women in Ulster Politics, 1890–1940: A History Not Yet Told* (Dublin: Irish Academic Press, 2002), p. 2.
[48] Ibid, pp. 60 and 102.
[49] Ibid., p. 61.
[50] Ibid., p. 72.
[51] Ibid., p. 73.
[52] Ulster Unionist Labour Association minutes, 3 July 1920 (PRONI, Ulster Unionist Council papers, D/1327/11/4/1).
[53] Diane Urquhart, *Women in Ulster Politics*, p. 122.

such as Lady Londonderry and Julia McMordie, were the figureheads for the mobilisation of women behind Ulster Unionism. McMordie was a candidate for Belfast Corporation in 1916 and was elected in 1918. She later also served in the Northern Ireland parliament. However, whilst auxiliary organisations for women were formed for Ulster Unionism and the Orange Order, this did not apply to the UULA. The Executive Committee of the UULA rejected women's membership in 1920, and given Craig's endorsement of that body in the 1930s, it was an unwise decision in the longer term. Political Unionism also endorsed the Victorian 'separate spheres' ideology: work was public, political and masculine, whereas the domestic and home life were feminine.

Irish Nationalists and republicans followed the dominant masculine assumptions of the inter-war period. Women's working conditions were an issue in Joe Devlin's west Belfast constituency. Many mills and factories were located there, and Devlin helped organise a hostel for holidays for young workers. Furthermore, in 1927, Devlin proposed enfranchising women on the same basis as men and eradicating the discriminatory franchise as it then stood. This was rejected by the UUP, only to be accepted the next year when the Westminster government proposed the amalgamation of the franchises of men and women. Irish Nationalist and Ulster Unionist politics was dominated by masculine assumptions, 'separate spheres' ideology. The next paragraphs delineate the biographies of some female left-wing activists in inter-war Belfast that subverted the social order.

A Scotch-born co-operator, Margaret T. McCoubrey, played an important role in local labour politics. She was born in Glasgow in 1880 and moved to Belfast in 1905. She became involved in labour, feminist and pacifist politics in Belfast and settled in Candahar Street, south Belfast. McCoubrey was also a member of the co-operative movement and was an executive member of the Co-Operative Guild in 1910–16. She was further an active member in the Independent Labour Party in Belfast and was elected for Dock ward in the 1920 Belfast Corporation elections. She continued as an important speaker, writer and organiser for the labour movement throughout the 1920s.[54] In the 1930s, she settled in Carnlough and ran a holiday home for the Belfast Girls' Club Union. This holiday home, and the Belfast Girls' Club Union, had a formative influence on Saidie

---

[54] Minute book of the Central Women's Section of the Northern Ireland Labour Party, 1924–32 (PRONI, D/3311/1).

Patterson. Saidie was involved in the Union and spent time at McCoubrey's holiday home. Saidie, in later years, remembered it fondly as a space for co-operation between working women and to combat sectarian division.[55] Both Mary Galway and M. T. McCoubrey point to the living tradition of female trade unionism which had been established by the inter-war period.

Winnifred Carney was a trade unionist, feminist, republican and labour activist. She was born in December 1887 in Bangor to a mixed marriage and became involved in the feminist and Gaelic movements in Belfast. She was appointed successor as secretary to Marie Johnson of the Belfast-based Irish Textile Workers' Union in 1912. Winnifred was also involved in the ITGWU and Cumann na mBan and was Connolly's aide-de-camp during the Easter Rising. She was subsequently arrested and became the first female candidate for election in Ulster at the 1918 general election. However, in a three-way contest, Carney came third with 539 votes (3.8%). Thomspon Donald (UULA) won with 9,309 votes (68.9%) to 3,469 votes (25.7%) for Robert Waugh of the Labour Representation Committee.[56] In 1920, she helped revive the Socialist Party of Ireland and was an anti-Treatyite during the Irish Civil War (1922–23). She continued to work for the ITGWU, was an active member of the Court Ward NILP branch and married a Protestant Ulster Volunteer Force ex-Serviceman, George McBride in 1928. She was also involved in the successor to the Independent Labour Party in Northern Ireland, the Socialist Party of Northern Ireland. But what was the wider significance of Carney's life?

Carney continued the work of James Connolly by combining republicanism and socialism. She subscribed to Connolly's aim of a Workers' Republic throughout her life and had the distinction of being the first female parliamentary candidate in Ulster's history. However, she received only 4% of the vote in 1918, and the UULA candidate in the same constituency received 10,000 votes. Victoria Ward, where Carney stood, included a small Catholic residential area, Short Strand, and the overwhelmingly Protestant east Belfast, so this helps to explain her modest vote. Carney's Court Ward Labour Party produced other important labour and communist activists during the inter-war period: Murtagh Morgan, Tommie Geehan, Ellen and James Grimley and Davey McClean,

---

[55] David Bleakley, *Saidie Patterson*, pp. 18–22.
[56] For the 1918 general election results in Ireland, see *Parliamentary Election Results in Ireland, 1800–1922* ed. by B. M. Walker (Dublin: Royal Irish Academy, 1978).

for example.[57] However, Winnifred does not seem to have played a role in the Central Women's Section of the NILP. Why, exactly, this was so remains unclear, but Carney was an example of a significant female republican-labour activist. Carney's career and life highlight how labour activists could undermine the gendered expectations of Belfast society. This subversion continued into the counter-revolutionary inter-war period.

Saidie Patterson was born in 1906 into a working-class household on the Shankill, Belfast. Her father was a devout Methodist and blacksmith; he died in 1912. The formative experience of Saidie's life was, however, the death of her mother on 13 December 1918. Saidie remembered that her family did not have enough money to call a doctor and this scarring experience had a dual effect on her life: Saidie had *both* a religious experience and a conversion to socialism.[58] Women in textiles were treated as an expendable commodity and suffered from industrial diseases.[59] Furthermore, textile workers often lived in tied housing, where the factory or mill owner had control of both housing and employment. Therefore, for many in the textile industry, to go on strike meant risking *both* income and home. Saidie was also involved in the Belfast Girls' Club Union, which was 'in [the] great tradition of late Victorian social service activity, with its provision of educational, recreational and holiday facilities for working girls'.[60] Saidie, however, most importantly, did not subscribe to the gendered conceptions of trade unionism she found:

> Instead of condemning the isolationist tendencies of the male trade unionists she encouraged them to widen the definition of their trade unionism, so that in the spirit of enlightened self-interest it would embrace their industrial sisters as well.[61]

It would take the seismic impact of the Second World War, however, before industrial relations in the region shifted considerably. The relationship of wartime and peacetime production in Ulster correlates with knowledge of trade unionism as pro-cyclical towards the wider economy.

[57] Helga Woggon, *Winnie Carney: A Silent Radical* (no date, no place of publication), pp. 16–17.
[58] Bleakley, *Saidie Patterson*, p. 12.
[59] Ibid., pp. 14–15.
[60] Ibid., p. 18.
[61] Ibid., p. 25.

In 1924, the year the NILP was founded, a Central Women's Section of the NILP was launched.[62] This was a vibrant section of the NILP for a number of years. But the close of the 1920s and early 1930s saw the end of a separate women's section of the NILP. What activities did the section conduct? They were involved in political and public meetings. For example, Labour MP Ellen Wilkinson spoke in Belfast on the 16 October 1925 to 1100 people and 240 copies of *Labour Woman* were sold.[63] When the British Trades Union Congress met in Belfast in 1929, the Central Women's Section of the NILP organised a women's meeting to coincide. The section was also involved in organising social events, cultural nights and educational meetings for members of the NILP. More seriously, perhaps, activists and members were also co-opted onto Belfast Corporation's Mother and Child Welfare Committee. The section was further involved in canvassing and helping with elections. However, the failure of the NILP to capitalise on elections locally in 1932 and at the Poor Law Board and Northern Ireland parliament elections in 1933 seems to have had a knock-on effect to the Central Women's Section. A major issue which appears continually in the minutes of the section is the lack of finance available to run candidates at elections.[64] The most significant aspect of this is that it was a specifically UUP decision in 1922 which increased the deposit necessary for local elections to £25 per candidate. This was a punitive cost for small political parties such as the NILP. The end of the Central Women's Section seems premature, as many of the issues highlighted by the section would be developed in later periods.

Betty Sinclair was the most well-known Belfast communist of the twentieth century, and in 2011 a street was renamed in her honour for International Women's Day. She was an important trade unionist for decades with the Belfast Trades Council and later chaired the Northern Ireland Civil Rights Association. She was born in 1910 to a working-class Church of Ireland household in north Belfast; her mother worked in the linen trade and her father at the shipyard. Betty's father was a supporter of William Walker. Sinclair joined the linen trade in 1925 and became interested in trade unionism and communism. In the early 1930s, she became involved with the Revolutionary Workers' Group in Belfast and played a

---

[62] See Minute book of the Central Women's Section of the Northern Ireland Labour Party, 1924–32 (PRONI, D/3311/1).
[63] Ibid.
[64] Ibid.

role in the Outdoor Relief riots of October 1932. She was a founding member of the Communist Party of Ireland, serving on its first Central Committee. She also spent two years at the International Lenin School (1933–35) and returned to Belfast in 1935. The next year she joined the Belfast Trades Council, representing linen workers, and continued to be involved in communist political activities. During the Second World War, Betty would first be imprisoned for printing republican material in the communist newspaper and stood as candidate for the Communist Party in the Cromac division, south Belfast, in 1945. There were important female activists in the labour movement during this period, but what about in local unionism?

The Victorian notion of 'separate spheres' ideology continued to be expressed explicitly and implicitly in Belfast during the inter-war period. In 1930, the UWUC, for example, claimed that the 'Poor Law work is women's work'.[65] However, women's political agency was also increasingly accepted. During the inter-war period in Belfast, however, women did play a limited political role in local governance and the Northern Ireland parliament. Three female MPs served for Northern Ireland in 1921–39. Whilst the numbers serving as Guardians was significantly higher, women were still significantly under-represented even in an area considered 'their' work. So women's political agency seems to have continued to be circumscribed by traditional gender conceptions during the inter-war period. Yet this is only a portion of the story as women were continuing to make cultural and political progress.

Women made further steps forward in the inter-war period when the most glaring inequality in the franchise, discrimination by age and sex, was removed with the 1928 Representation of the People Act. This act enfranchised women in Northern Ireland on the same basis as men in the UK. However, in Northern Ireland, the local UUP administration passed a number of extra amendments. Alongside changes in local government in 1922, the 1929 Representation of the People Act introduced a UK residency qualification of three years for Northern Ireland voters.[66] The Act also created a business franchise for Northern Ireland Parliamentary

[65] Quoted in Diane Urquhart, '"The Female of the Species is More Deadlier than the Male?" The Ulster Women's Unionist Council, 1911–40', in *Coming into the Light: The Work, Politics and Religion of Women in Ulster, 1840–1940* ed. by Janice Holmes and Diane Urquhart (Belfast: Queen's University Belfast Institute of Irish Studies, 1994), pp. 93–123 (p. 111).
[66] See footnote 46, Chap. 1.

elections and local elections. The 1929 Act, owing to the wealth disparities between the confessional denominations, also favoured the wealthier,
Protestant, sections of Northern Ireland society. The supremacy created
by the UUP in Northern Ireland consisted of coercive law, dominance and
political control. But, given the necessity of coercion and repressive law, it
seems more accurate to describe inter-war Northern Ireland as a 'dominance without hegemony'.[67]

The importance of the female vote is exemplified by the 1928 cartoon,
'On Whom Will She Smile?', which illustrated the opening of this chapter.
Despite the economic, legal and cultural restrictions women faced, they
were still developing their own political agency. The 'Queen of the May's
choice is limited to either Unionist or Opposition. This binary political
choice summates the concept of a moral economy of loyalty in Northern
Ireland. Such politics was the expression of the political control and social
order created by the UUP administration of Northern Ireland. However,
to call the governance of Northern Ireland 'hegemonic' is a misnomer.
The UUP dominated Northern Ireland, but this was not hegemonic and
is closer to Guha's conception of British rule in India: a 'dominance without hegemony'. Women's political agency in Northern Ireland may have
been traditional in many senses, but this also included significant aspects
of their choice and agency. However, rather than judge feminine political
agency, the present author considers it more worthwhile to examine the
social, cultural, economic and political context, alongside the acts of political choice made by women: they lived in this era, after all, and we did not.

5.6   MEN, WOMEN AND THE POLITICS OF GENDER

Women continued to face a number of difficult political, social, cultural
and economic issues during the inter-war period. However, a number of
analyses related to gender and masculinity in inter-war Northern Ireland
have appeared recently. J.G.V. McGaughey, for example, has investigated
Protestant Unionist masculinities in the region in 1912–23.[68] In this
book, McGaughey investigates the construction of a hegemonic masculinity in the region. The First World War, according to McGaughey, was

---

[67] The term is taken from an important piece of Indian Subaltern Studies, Ranajit Guha,
Dominance without Hegemony: History and Power in Colonial India (Cambridge, MA:
Harvard University Press, 1997).

[68] See footnote 4 above.

the key event in the construction of a regional hegemony. However, the use of 'hegemony' is questionable in the analysis conducted by McGaughey. At the same time that she illuminates the 'hegemony' of Protestant Unionist masculinities, she is forced to continually highlight the rejection of these conceptions by Irish nationalists, separatists, Catholics, labour and other disloyalists. 'Hegemony', in the Gramscian sense, is dominance without coercion and therefore the UUP's administration of Northern Ireland lacked hegemony. The UUP administration of government in the region was obliged to make use of coercion rather than consent. The use of the Special Powers Act, electoral malpractice and the existence of unreconciled minorities illustrates the 'dominance without hegemony' that was the moral economy of loyalty. If the UUP, or Protestant Unionist masculinities, had been 'hegemonic', then there would have been no necessity of politics as a police action.[69] A similar problematic is at work in Brady's article on gender in inter-war Northern Ireland.

In Sean Brady's recent article on religion and masculinities in Northern Ireland, there is a similar issue with the utilisation of the term 'hegemony'. For Brady, inter-war Northern Ireland consisted of competing 'masculine hegemonies'.[70] Some of the difficulty with the term can be illustrated by the claim that Catholic masculinity could be *both* hegemonic and counterhegemonic.[71] The 'hegemonic masculinities' Brady is examining are, I would argue, the exhibition of the commonality of 'separate spheres' ideology within both Ulster Unionism and Irish Nationalism. The misuse of 'hegemony' is, however, a common misappropriation of the term. Hegemony means rule by consent: in other words, it is about the creation of agreed frameworks. Both women and Labour, though to differing extents, were assimilated to British and Irish society during the inter-war period. Over-emphasis on hegemonic masculinity is in danger of causing us to discount the evidence of female labour activists such as Carney, Galway, McCoubrey, Sinclair and Patterson detailed above. What remains to be explained, however, is the inability of the UUP to construct a viable hegemonic apparatus in Northern Ireland.

Diane Urquhart, the historian of women's unionism, concludes that during the inter-war period, 'women were treated as a form of surplus

[69] Jacques Rancière, *Disagreement: Politics and Philosophy*, p. xiii.
[70] Brady, 'Why Examine Men, Masculinities and Religion in Northern Ireland?', p. 223.
[71] See Brady, 'Why Examine Men, Masculinities and Religion in Northern Ireland?'.

population, largely forced out of the workplace and back into the home'.[72] The UWUC, with its traditional conception of women's work, largely conformed to British experience during the inter-war period. However, by the 1930s, women did have equal political rights. Yet this had not successfully eroded 'separate spheres' ideology and women continued to suffer legal, economic and cultural obstacles. Some of the counter-revolutions experienced by women during the inter-war period were therefore accompanied by progressive developments. For example, the viability of women's trade unionism was definitively proven during the inter-war period, in both Ireland and Britain. There was also the continued significance of female employment. But, significantly, the lack of munitions work in Ireland during the First World War, alongside the different experience of conscription and manpower, may have resulted in less dislocation in the immediate post-war period. Alongside this Janus-faced experience can be set the record of women in the trade unions in Ireland.

During the inter-war period, women became increasingly visible in the Irish trade union movement.[73] These developments were apparent through the contribution of feminist and labour voices to debates related to the development of De Valera's Ireland, the constitution of 1937 and employment and vocationalism. In 1923, younger women in southern Ireland were enfranchised on the same basis as men, five years before Northern Ireland and the UK. This acceptance of women as equal citizens must have played some role in stopping the complete acceptance of 'separate spheres' ideology within inter-war Ireland. With the onset of the Second World War in 1939, women in Northern Ireland would soon be in a position to demand better conditions. In 1940, for example, Saidie Patterson led a two-month strike against the 'Linen Lords' of Belfast as represented by Ewart's Mill. Betty Sinclair would also invigorate feminism and campaign for women to play their role in the fight versus fascism. Furthermore, in 1943, the Standing Committee of Women's Organisations, acting as a forum for women and feminists to interact, was formed in Belfast. This evidence, again, points away from any simplistic notion of a 'hegemonic masculinity' in Northern Ireland.

---

[72] Diane Urquhart, '"The Female of the Species is More Deadlier than the Male"?', p. 115.
[73] See the sections on women's trade unionism in *Trade Union Century* ed. by Donal Nevin (Dublin: Mercier Press, 1994).

5.7   CONCLUSION

The social and economic conditions which faced working women in inter-war Belfast were difficult. They were paid less for the same labour as men and suffered legal discrimination via marriage bars and a lack of public healthcare related to maternal and child welfare. They had, however, obtained an equal franchise with men by 1928 in Northern Ireland, southern Ireland and the UK. It was also increasingly accepted that women could work for wages, and the viability of female trade unionism within the labour movement had been demonstrated. Culturally, 'separate spheres' ideology was still dominant in Belfast and Northern Ireland, but this was attenuated by the progressive development of political and cultural rights for women. This shift is exemplified by the cartoon introduced at the beginning of the chapter, 'The Queen of the May, 1929: On Whom Will She Smile?' The young woman illustrated in the cartoon clearly demonstrates agency and choice. The modernism of the representation is striking: straight silhouette rather than the fashion of wide hips of the Victorian and Edwardian eras; a short 'bob' hair-cut rather than long curls; her skirt cut above the knee rather than long to the ankle. The picture subverts the 'separate spheres' ideology of women as domestic and non-political. Such subversion, however, does not outweigh the evidence of cultural, economic and social constriction which faced women.

Politically, women made important steps forward during the inter-war period. This role is explicitly demonstrated in Ulster Unionist, Irish Nationalist and Labour politics in Belfast. The labour movement also had important female political personalities. The Central Women's Section of the NILP was an admirable, if unsuccessful, attempt to cater to female political activism. However, both the UWUC and the Central Women's Section of the NILP dealt with issues which reflected the dominant masculine assumptions of inter-war Belfast. For the UUP, this was the import of calling Poor Law work 'women's work'.[74] Last, the sample of left-wing female activism points to the subversion available for female political agency in Belfast. Galway, McCoubrey, Carney, Patterson and Sinclair were all radicals in their respective fields. They refused, for example, to accept that the labour movement should exclude women. In conclusion, women, politically, did not uphold or propagate 'hegemonic

---

[74] See footnote 65 above.

masculinities' in any simple fashion. The inter-war period was an epoch of victorious counter-revolutions and institutionalisation of these forms of politics. Yet, owing to the advancements made by women, the Northern Ireland regime of the inter-war period should also be understood as a relatively *democratised ancien régime*.

CHAPTER 6

Conclusion: Belfast Labour, Civil Rights and the Politics of Disloyalty

Abstract The case studies demonstrate that a moral economy of loyalty was the 'rules of the game' in Belfast and Northern Ireland politics in 1921–39. Essentially, Labour and class politics could not have overturned the Ulster Unionist Party's dominance. Decisions made in London resulted in a regionalised state and a peculiar political culture. In this regionalised culture, the power holders became self-perpetuating and utilised an essentially plebiscitary democracy. This ensured a secure state by 1939. Labour in Belfast in 1921–39 was a victim, alongside Catholics, Irish Nationalists and Republicans, of the moral economy of loyalty constructed in the region. The moral economy of loyalty resulted in a society controlled by domination and coercion rather than hegemony.

Keywords Belfast • Disloyalty • Labour • Loyalty • Moral economy

The case studies presented above began as a PhD thesis on the political culture of the Belfast labour movement of 1924–39. A central conclusion of that thesis was that labour failed in Belfast but did also register some success.[1] As is clear from the above case studies, this book makes a substantially different claim. The case studies demonstrate that, essentially,

---

[1] C. J. V. Loughlin, 'The Political Culture of the Belfast Labour Movement, 1924–39' (unpublished PhD thesis, Queen's University Belfast, 2013).

© The Author(s) 2018
C. J. V. Loughlin, *Labour and the Politics of Disloyalty in Belfast, 1921–39*, https://doi.org/10.1007/978-3-319-71081-5_6

141

labour and class politics could not have won. Decisions made in London resulted in a regionalised state and a peculiar political culture. In this regionalised culture, the power holders became self-perpetuating, utilising an essentially plebiscitary democracy. The self-perpetuating nature of the regime and its supposed democratic credentials ensured a secure state by 1939. The security of the state in Belfast and Northern Ireland, however, rested on coercion and not consent. The local Unionist administration is best described, therefore, as a 'dominance without hegemony'.[2] The politics of the Irish *ancien régime* lived on in a democratised and counter-revolutionary form. This regime was relatively successful in the creation of law and order; it was much less successful in creating a loyal political culture. The politics of disloyalty was the means by which non-loyalists were excluded from full participation in Northern Ireland. The politics of disloyalty is how the moral economy of loyalty was expressed for opponents of the Ulster Unionist Party (UUP) regime.

Labour in Belfast between 1921 and 1939 was the main victim, alongside Catholics, Irish Nationalists and republicans, of this moral economy of loyalty. Supporters of the labour movement were susceptible to conflict, violence and intimidation because of their disloyalty. Amongst the Ulster Unionist elite, the paramount question was identifying loyal friends and disloyal enemies. In this moral economy of loyalty, Labour could not have won. Furthermore, Labour's roots in workplace politics and internationalist ideologies made them suspect to the local elite. As such, the relative inability of the local labour movement to deal with sectarianism and nationalism becomes explicable. Marxism, the most consistent and coherent left-wing ideology yet produced, similarly failed to develop a consistent position on either of these issues. Northern Ireland, Labour and Marxism have all yet to fundamentally resolve these topics. The contemporary failure on these issues is therefore matched by historical failure. This knowledge should make us pause for thought before we judge Belfast Labour too harshly; we are liable to forget that we are not at the end of historical evolution either. The above case studies, perhaps, point to the insolubility of such conflict: a resolution of these issues may not be possible, merely recognition or amelioration. In electoral politics, we saw how Labour was able to mobilise a substantial vote, but this was significantly under-represented during the inter-war period.

---

[2] Ranajit Guha, *Dominance without Hegemony: History and Power in Colonial India* (Cambridge, MA: Harvard University Press, 1997).

In 1921, when Northern Ireland was established, single transferable vote proportional representation was utilised for both local and parliamentary elections. In 1920, labour supporters had gained over 20,000 votes and one sixth of Belfast Corporation seats. The reversion to simple plurality for the 1923 Belfast urban election resulted in a similar vote, but only two councillors returned. Furthermore, the abolition of proportional representation and reversion to 1898 ward boundaries resulted in the long-term decline of electoral competition on Belfast Corporation. A similar problem occurred with the return to simple plurality for the 1929 parliament election: the decline of electoral competition, unopposed wins and a supposed monolithic and hegemonic Ulster Unionism. Despite these problems, Labour maintained a political presence and vote in Belfast. This vote expanded dramatically during the Second World War, alongside trade unionism. The entrenched power, coercion and control exercised by the elite in Northern Ireland, however, meant that Belfast Labour could not have successfully challenged Ulster Unionism. The only viable political option available was a coalition of anti-Unionist forces. Yet co-operation between anti-Unionist forces during the inter-war period continually broke down. It would require significant change of the wider and local context to challenge Ulster Unionism: the 'long' civil rights movement and the radical 1960s.

6.1   Loyalty and the Democratic Ancien Régime, 1921–39

Northern Ireland, by 1939, had been successfully established as a state. However, partition and the establishment of the state created a number of injustices which were compounded by successive governments. The establishment of a moral economy of loyalty also created a number of losers in the political game: Irish Nationalists, republicans, separatists, Gaelic activists, Catholics and left-wing groups were all considered disloyal and liable to discriminatory action. Law, culture and society became permeated by a zero-sum game of loyalty and disloyalty, or a moral economy of loyalty. The rules of the electoral game were legislated first at Westminster in 1920 and subsequently locally. These rules facilitated a majoritarian, or plebiscitary, democracy that consistently hindered the emergence, and sustainability, of opposition to the UUP. Similar exclusionist legislation affected the administration of unemployment benefits, and after the Second World

War the scope of such laws was expanded. Electoral success, the administration of the state and the use of special powers all contributed to what appeared to be a monolithic regime by 1939. The lack of hegemony of the UUP regime, however, highlights the necessity of coercion and emergency law to consolidate the state.

The regime established in Northern Ireland, with Belfast as the new state's capital, was coercive and not hegemonic. An excessively centralised and powerful state was created in Northern Ireland. But the regime established was shaped by crisis, war and revolution. These events, not discounting other issues, saw a peculiar regime created: both aristocratic and bourgeois, it was dominated by conceptions of loyalty, Protestantism and Unionism. Furthermore, these injustices institutionalised grievance at the heart of the state and political culture. Section five of the Government of Ireland Act (1920) may have contributed to this politicisation of the state. The prohibition of religious endorsement or penalty, alongside other democratic reforms, was supposed to ensure the equitable running of Northern Ireland. But the politicisation of the state may have been an unintended consequence of such well-meaning attempts to stop inter-religious competition. The result was that *de jure* Northern Ireland could be considered an ordinary liberal democracy; *de facto*, it was a Protestant political and cultural economy. The moral economy of loyalty was the political form through which such an old tradition of inter-confessional rivalry could be expressed in the new context of mass democracy. It was, however, only with special pleading that Northern Ireland could be considered within the spirit of the 1920 Government of Ireland Act. The moral economy of loyalty was the coercive dominance, without hegemony, of the regime in Northern Ireland. How did the Belfast labour movement deal with these issues?

6.2   Civil Liberties, Labour and the 'Long' Civil Rights Movement, 1921–39

The Belfast labour movement in 1921–39 successfully maintained a viable electoral, organisational and political force. Left-wing forces in the city continued to marshal significant numbers of members and votes despite being continually under-represented by simple plurality voting. Belfast Labour contributed significantly to democratic and left-wing developments in Ireland pre-1914 and this continued during the inter-war period.

Marxism, for example, developed extensively in the Atlantic world pre-1914. James Connolly's time in Belfast in 1910–14 is exemplary in this regard, and William Walker also played a supporting role. But Marxism was relatively under-developed in relation to both nationalism and sectarianism; the situation was little changed during the 1920s and 1930s. But Marxists, socialists and communists all contributed to the Belfast labour movement during the inter-war period. In the unemployment struggle of both decades, left-wing activists played a leadership role. Left-wing groups also agitated against the use of emergency powers legislation, for example, during the investigation conducted by the National Council for Civil Liberties in 1935 and 1936. They were also a significant influence on wider progressive and feminist politics. This is demonstrated in Winnifred Carney's and Betty Sinclair's respective careers within the labour movement and progressive politics. The Belfast labour movement in 1921–39 was a precursor to the establishment of the civil rights movement in Northern Ireland in the 1960s. It cannot be fully delineated here, but the Belfast labour movement did make a substantial contribution to the 'long' civil rights movement. Future publications, by the present author, will investigate this topic in more detail.

The creation of the Northern Ireland state was a politically contentious decision and remains a source of instability. The decision to partition the island left unresolved democratic, social and political issues. Furthermore, the use of coercion was compounded by the decision to re-introduce simple plurality voting for local elections. Similar legislation on unemployment benefits meant that these areas involved civil rights (or 'civil liberties' as they were referred to during the inter-war period). Political co-operation between the opposition was the nightmare scenario of the Belfast elite. Such collaboration did occur during both the 1920s and 1930s but never developed further during the period under consideration. In 1929, the re-introduction of simple plurality voting ended co-operation between the left and Irish Nationalism, and, in 1936, the Spanish Civil War sabotaged further co-operation by the same forces in Belfast. It was only in the 1960s that the civil rights movement provided an arena for sustained co-operation between forces opposed to the UUP.

Sectarianism, Christian-based ethno-national conflict, was the key dividing line in Northern Ireland. But religion was an old and colonial tradition by the early twentieth century in the north of Ireland. The nineteenth century had witnessed urbanisation and industrialisation in Belfast and the Lagan Valley. Similarly, the beginning of democracy and renewed imperialist developments took place in the second half of the nineteenth century. The politics of crisis, war, revolution and counter-revolution were refracted through these lenses. We should therefore be careful not to essentialise religious sectarianism in Belfast. Sectarianism was not a master card, or trick, which inevitably defeated Labour or class politics. Religion has contended with labour and left-wing politics; this is not a unique Atlantic, British, global or Irish phenomenon. The resolution of such issues is also still not at an end. What we can say for certain is that religion played a key role in Belfast's inter-war politics, although this was expressed through a moral economy of loyalty due to the legislation and events which accompanied the foundation of Northern Ireland. Belfast's politics was not dominated explicitly by religious difference; it appears that section five of the Government of Ireland Act (1920), not excluding other issues, politicised the administration of the state and the public-private space. Local society, as a result, became heavily weighted towards the majority community via a moral economy of loyalty.

Index[1]

[1]Note: Page number followed by 'n' refer to notes.

© The Author(s) 2018   147
C. J. V. Loughlin, *Labour and the Politics of Disloyalty in Belfast,*
1921–39, https://doi.org/10.1007/978-3-319-71081-5

CPI Antony Rowe
Eastbourne, UK
April 23, 2019